# A Tribute to Peter Bauer

# A Tribute to Peter Bauer

INCLUDING A CONVERSATION WITH PETER BAUER
AND TRIBUTES BY JOHN BLUNDELL,
JAMES M. BUCHANAN, MEGHNAD DESAI,
JAMES A. DORN, RALPH HARRIS, DEEPAK LAL,
VICTORIA CURZON PRICE, RAZEEN SALLY,
PARTH J. SHAH, ALAN WALTERS AND BASIL YAMEY

The Institute of Economic Affairs

First published in Great Britain in 2002 by
The Institute of Economic Affairs
2 Lord North Street
Westminster
London SW1P 3LB
in association with Profile Books Ltd

A CIP catalogue record for this book is available from the British Library.

ISBN 0 255 36531 4

Many IEA publications are translated into languages other than English or
are reprinted. Permission to translate or to reprint should be sought from the
General Director at the address above.

Typeset in Stone by MacGuru
info@macguru.org.uk

Printed and bound in Great Britain by Hobbs the Printers

# CONTENTS

# THE AUTHORS

## John Blundell

John Blundell is General Director of the Institute of Economic Affairs. He was educated at King's School, Macclesfield, and at the London School of Economics. He headed the Press, Research and Parliamentary Liaison Office at the Federation of Small Businesses from 1977 to 1982. From 1982 to 1993 he lived in the US where he was, *inter alia*, President of the Institute for Humane Studies (1988–91); President of the Atlas Economic Research Foundation (1987–91); President of the board of the Congressional Schools of Virginia (1988–92); and President of the Charles G. Koch and Claude R. Lambe Charitable Foundations (1991–2).

He assumed his duties as General Director of the Institute of Economic Affairs on 1 January 1993. He also served as co-founder and chairman, from 1993 to 1997, of the Institute for Children, Boston, Mass.; founder director (1991–3), Institute for Justice, Washington, DC; international trustee (1988–93), The Fraser Institute, Vancouver, BC; and founder trustee of Buckeye Institute, Dayton, Ohio.

He is a director of Fairbridge and of International Policy Network and chairman of the executive committee of the board of Atlas Economic Research Foundation (USA). He is also a board member of the Institute for Humane Studies at George Mason

University, Fairfax, Va.; of the Institute of Economic Studies (Europe) in Paris, France; and of the Mont Pélerin Society.

## James M. Buchanan

James Buchanan was born on 3 October 1919 in Murfreesboro, Tenn. He remains Advisory General Director, Center for Study of Public Choice, George Mason University, Fairfax, Va., even though he retired in 1999 as Distinguished Professor Emeritus of Economics from George Mason University and University Distinguished Professor Emeritus of Economics and Philosophy from Virginia Polytechnic and State University, Blacksburg, Va. Professor Buchanan received his BA from Middle Tennessee State College in 1940; his MS from the University of Tennessee in 1941; and his PhD from the University of Chicago in 1948. In 1986, Professor Buchanan received the Alfred Nobel Memorial Prize in Economic Sciences. The following is a short list of his most well-known major works: *The Collected Works of James M. Buchanan* (20 vols, 1999–2002, 2004); *Better than Plowing: And Other Personal Essays* (1992); *The Economics and the Ethics of Constitutional Order* (1991); *The Reason of Rules* (with Geoffrey Brennan, 1985); *The Power to Tax* (with Geoffrey Brennan, 1980); *Freedom in Constitutional Contract* (1978); *Democracy in Deficit* (with Richard E. Wagner, 1977); *Liberty, Market and State* (1975); *The Limits of Liberty* (1975); *The Calculus of Consent* (with Gordon Tullock, 1962).

## Meghnad Desai

Born in India, Meghnad Desai is Professor of Economics and Director of the Centre for the Study of Global Governance at the

London School of Economics. He became Lord Desai of St Clement Danes in 1991. He has honorary degrees from the Universities of East London, Guildhall, Kingston and Middlesex. His most recent publication is *Marx's Revenge: The Resurgence of Capitalism and Death of Statist Socialism*.

## James A. Dorn

James Dorn is vice-president for academic affairs at the Cato Institute, editor of the *Cato Journal*, and director of Cato's annual monetary conference. His research interests include trade and human rights, economic reform in China, and the future of money. He directed Cato's Project on Civil Society from 1993 to 1995. From 1984 to 1990, he served on the White House Commission on Presidential Scholars. He has edited ten books, including *The Revolution in Development Economics* (with Steve Hanke and Alan Walters), and his articles have appeared in numerous publications. He has been a visiting scholar at the Central European University in Prague and at Fudan University in Shanghai, and is currently professor of economics at Towson University in Maryland. Dorn holds an MA and a PhD in economics from the University of Virginia.

## Ralph Harris

Ralph Harris was born in London in 1924, graduated from Cambridge in 1947, taught at St Andrews University, stood unsuccessfully for Parliament in 1951 and 1955, and wrote for the *Glasgow Herald*, before returning to London in 1957 to launch Antony Fisher's Institute of Economic Affairs as General Director of the first of the 'think tanks'. With Arthur Seldon as Editorial Director, the IEA published a stream of student texts by authors (including Hayek, Friedman, Buchanan and many others prepared to 'think the unthinkable') who helped rehabilitate the classical liberal tradition of market analysis from the ravages of Keynesian conservatism and socialism. He formally retired in 1989. In 1979, when Margaret Thatcher became Prime Minister, Ralph Harris was made a life peer as Lord Harris of High Cross and sits (occasionally) in the House of Lords as a non-party 'cross-bencher'.

## Deepak Lal

Deepak Lal is James S. Coleman Professor of International Development Studies, University of California at Los Angeles, and Professor Emeritus of Political Economy, University College, London. He has been a member of the Indian Foreign Service, Lecturer, Jesus College, Oxford, and Christ Church, Oxford, Research Fellow, Nuffield College, Oxford, Lecturer and Reader in Political Economy, University College, London, and Professor of Political Economy, University of London. He was a full-time consultant to the Indian Planning Commission from 1973 to 1974, and has served as a consultant to the ILO, UNCTAD, OECD, UNIDO, the World Bank, and the ministries of planning in South Korea and Sri Lanka. During 1983–4 he was an Economic Adviser to the World Bank, and then Research Administrator (1984–7), on leave from University College, London.

Professor Lal is the author of numerous articles and books on economic development and public policy, including, for the IEA, *The Poverty of 'Development Economics'*, Hobart Paper 144 (revised edition 2002), *The Limits of International Cooperation* (Occasional Paper 83), and *The Minimum Wage* (Occasional Paper 95).

## Victoria Curzon Price

Victoria Curzon Price is Professor of Economics at the University of Geneva, and a member of the Academic Advisory Council of the IEA and of the Centre for the New Europe, Brussels. She is a member of the Board and Vice President of the Mont Pélerin Society. She was Director of the European Institute of the University of Geneva, a faculty member of the International Management Institute and a visiting professor at the University of Amsterdam. Professor Curzon Price is the author of many books and articles on international trade policy and European integration. Her most recent publications include *The Enlargement of the European Union: Issues and Strategies* (co-editor with Alice Landau and Richard G. Whitman, 1999); 'Industrial policy in the European Union: the control of state aid and support for R&D' (chapter in El-Agraa, ed., *The Economics of the European Community*, 2001); 'Some causes and consequences of fragmentation' (in Kierzkowski & Arndt, eds., *Fragmentation and International Trade*, 2001); and 'How to become a rich country: lessons from Switzerland' (in Gissurarson, H. H. and Herbertsson, T. T., eds., *Tax Competition: An opportunity for Iceland?*, 2001).

## Razeen Sally

Razeen Sally is Senior Lecturer in International Political Economy at the London School of Economics and Political Science, where he has taught since 1993, and head of its International Trade Policy Unit. He is a Visiting Professor at the Institut d'Etudes Politiques in Paris, and at Tallinn Technical University in Estonia; and a Visiting Senior Research Fellow at the Institute of Southeast Asian Studies, Singapore. From 1992 to

1993, he was a Research Fellow at the European Institute of Business Administration (INSEAD) in Fontainebleau, France, and was a Visiting Professor at Dartmouth College in the USA in 1998. Dr Sally received his PhD from the LSE in 1992, having previously studied at the University of Frankfurt, the Free University of Berlin, and the European University Institute in Florence, Italy. His research has focused on trade policy-making in developing and transitional countries, notably in eastern Europe and East Asia, and on developing country participation in the WTO. He also writes on the intellectual history of political economy, especially the theory of commercial policy in the classical liberal tradition.

### Parth J. Shah

Parth J. Shah received his Bachelor of Pharmacy degree from Maharaja Sayajirao University, Vadodara, India, and a PhD in economics (with a special emphasis on Austrian political economy) from Auburn University in the US. He taught economics at the University of Michigan-Dearborn before returning to India in August 1997 to start the Centre for Civil Society, a free-market think tank in Delhi. He has published academic articles in the areas of development economics, welfare economics, business cycle theory, free or laissez-faire banking, and currency board systems. Since then, his research has focused on the provision of social services and the role of private initiative in that sector. He is the editor of *Friedman on India, Profiles in Courage: Dissent on Indian Socialism*, and *Do Corporations Have Social Responsibility?* He is a regular columnist with the *Economic Times*. He enjoys applying economic principles to the understanding of human and non-human behaviour, and is always engaged in economics except when he plays chess, badminton or tennis.

## Alan Walters

Alan Walters is known mainly in his role as Chief Economic Adviser to the Prime Minister during the 1980s. He has held chairs of econometrics, statistics and economics at Birmingham, the London School of Economics and Johns Hopkins. In his academic work he has contributed mainly in the fields of statistical production functions, pricing policies for state-owned assets (particularly road pricing), and monetary economics. In policy work he has advised international financial institutions and various finance ministers and central banks. Throughout the 1990s he was vice-president of AIG International.

## Basil Yamey

Basil Yamey graduated from the University of Cape Town, where he later taught, before he joined the staff of the London School of Economics in 1947. He was appointed Professor of Economics at LSE in 1960. Also in 1960 he wrote for the IEA its first Hobart Paper – *Resale Price Maintenance and Shopper's Choice* – a book which many people believe was very influential in the abolition of resale price maintenance in Britain. He was for many years a member of the IEA's Academic Advisory Council. He has written on the economics of retailing, on the economics of industrial structure, on the economics and law of monopoly and restrictive practices, on commodity markets and futures exchanges, and on the history of accounting, and he was Peter Bauer's collaborator and co-author in writing about the economics of developing countries.

# FOREWORD

Professor Peter Bauer (Lord Bauer of Market Ward) died on 2 May 2002 at the age of 86. This volume is a tribute to the work of an economist who had considerable influence on economic policy – in particular, on the prevailing wisdom about foreign aid ('government-to-government transfers', as he preferred to call it).

Evidence of the regard in which Peter was held, and the scale of his achievements, is provided by his receipt of the first $500,000 Milton Friedman Prize for Advancing Liberty, awarded by the Cato Institute in Washington, DC. Peter was given this prestigious award just before his death and was due to have travelled to Washington for the formal presentation at the 25th Anniversary Dinner of the Cato Institute on 9 May 2002.

This Occasional Paper begins with a transcript of a conversation between Lord Bauer and John Blundell, General Director of the Institute of Economic Affairs. The transcript is taken from a video, produced by the Liberty Fund of Indianapolis, Indiana, in its Intellectual Portraits series, and is reproduced here by kind permission of the Liberty Fund. It provides an insight into how Peter Bauer saw his own career, his interactions with other economists, and his contributions to economic analysis.

There follows a speech by John Blundell, made at the presentation of the Milton Friedman Prize mentioned above. The award ceremony went ahead in Washington on 9 May, after Peter's death. At the end of his speech, and also reproduced here, Blundell read out the acceptance speech which Peter had already written.

The remaining sections of this Occasional Paper contain ten tributes to Peter Bauer, written by eminent economists who knew him well, who appreciated his influence and who saw his work from different perspectives. They provide an appraisal of the life and work of a great economist whose writings have had a fundamental effect on the economics of development.

As in all IEA publications, the views expressed in this Occasional Paper are those of the authors, not of the Institute (which has no corporate view), its managing trustees, Academic Advisory Council members or senior staff.

COLIN ROBINSON
*Editorial Director, Institute of Economic Affairs*
*Professor of Economics, University of Surrey*
August 2002

# A Tribute to Peter Bauer

# 1 A CONVERSATION WITH PETER BAUER

## Introduction

Pieter Thomas Bauer was born in Budapest, Hungary, in 1915, and came to the UK to study at Cambridge in the 1930s.

Ultimately his economic views turned him in a direction quite different from that of the Keynesian school of thought so prevalent in Cambridge in that era. Instead, he developed a more laissez-faire conviction. In the mid-1940s, he published an initial work on the rubber industries in Malaya, which began the formulation of his views on economic development, views that were expanded and built upon over 40 years of prolific writing.

Lord Bauer's thinking presented a new view of the role of government intervention in the development of Third World economies. His work illustrated that private entrepreneurs were more likely to be engines of development, and that Western aid was often more likely to perpetuate poor government policies and corruption than foster true economic vitality.

Lord Bauer taught at the London School of Economics from 1960 to 1983. In 1983, he became a life peer in recognition of his distinguished service. And throughout his career he devoted himself, in writing and in thought, to furthering the understanding of how best to develop a prosperous economy while maintaining individual freedom.

## The conversation

Lord Peter Bauer (PB)
John Blundell (JB)

JB: I understand that, as a teenager, you enrolled for law school, you became a law student.

PB: Well, I just finished secondary education. I then went to Budapest University where I had a year before going to Cambridge.

JB: It has intrigued me. How could a teenaged law student from Budapest find his way across Europe and enrol to study economics at Cambridge in 1934? How did that come about?

PB: My late father was a bookmaker. One of his clients, a great Anglophile, suggested my father provide an English education for his very hard-working and, apparently, quite talented son, so that's how I came to be at Cambridge.

JB: So you turned up at Cambridge and you went knocking door to door, college to college? What was the reaction? How did they receive you?

PB: All very friendly, but they were surprised, they were surprised. In fact, I presented myself at six colleges, and five accepted me immediately, and the sixth the next day.

JB: Of what standard was your English?

PB: It was awful. I had a very difficult time at Cambridge, because I was very short of money and I hardly spoke any English.

JB: And what led you to choose economics as a discipline?

PB: Because I thought that eventually I would return to Hungary and practise private international law. Because I thought law and economics would be helpful.

JB: How did you move over the years, as you say, from being mildly on the left to being a great champion of market ideas and limited government and so on?

PB: Simply reflection and observation. The prevailing thought among undergraduates in Cambridge at the time was very much on the left. And a great deal of respect for the Soviet Union. I maintained at the time already that in a country in which there's ultimately only one employer there cannot be a free society.

JB: You've raised the issue of the Soviet Union. How did you feel about its demise a decade ago now?

PB: I was convinced that it wouldn't last, but I never believed that it would disintegrate so rapidly. I thought it would eventually go, the system was so inefficient, prices so divorced from the real costs of production. The system would have to go, but I never thought that it would have to go so soon, without a shot being fired.

JB: Planning in that case, central government planning, clearly didn't work. What does this tell us, do you think, about your own field of Third World development, where many different forms of planning have been tried?

PB: Much the same. Central planning is something which I think is inherently in error. Whether in the Third World or in the West.

JB: It's doomed to failure?

PB: Well, it depends on how you define failure. If you mean failure in improving living standards or promoting economic progress, yes. If it is a question of keeping the government in power, that's a different story. In the Third World even more than in the West, the primary aim of any government is to stay in power.

JB: Let's talk a little more about Cambridge in the 1930s. Were you actually taught by Joan Robinson and Maynard Keynes?

PB: Yes, I attended a few of Keynes' lectures. He didn't give many lectures, he gave a few lectures. I was a member of the society called the Keynes Club, which met at Keynes' room twice a term, consisting of some dons and some promising undergraduates. I was a member of that and Joan Robinson supervised me for a year.

JB: So six times a year, twice a term, the brightest students and faculty would meet at Keynes' house as part of the Keynes Club to discuss ideas?

PB: Yes. Somebody would present a paper and that was then discussed. It was all really rigged by Kahn. You see, Kahn sent out slips of paper to students or members of the club whom he wanted to talk, and we had to talk. I was not very articulate in those days.

JB: So Kahn would rig it for people that he wanted to promote?

PB: Yes. That was not malicious. I mean, someone with just something to contribute, or due to speak. So during the paper they came up to speak.

JB: What was it like having Joan Robinson as your tutor?

PB: That was something quite different. She was a very good supervisor. She was my supervisor, but she gradually came very much to dislike me because I was then becoming market oriented, and she was totally hostile to the market.

JB: Did you set out to change the world?

PB: I was very naive in those days. I did want to change certain things which, oddly enough, I did manage to change. For instance, I thought the smallholders were very unfairly treated by property regulation, and I criticised this very effectively, and that has changed policy in Malaya definitely.

JB: You are often called a market-oriented economist, yet people say markets produce great inequalities. How do you deal with such an accusation?

PB: First of all, I would say we shouldn't talk about inequalities, but differences, because difference is a neutral term, and inequality is a loaded term. Inequalities often are equated with inequity. Except this leads to the idea that the poor are poor because the rich are rich, i.e. that the rich have extracted their incomes or wealth from the poor, which is not true.

JB: What does lead to these great differences, then?

PB: The most important thing, I suppose, is the difference in economic abilities. You see, people accept the idea that people differ greatly in athletic ability, musical ability and mathematical ability; but people don't seem to realise that there are also great differences in economic qualities, particularly in the perception and utilisation of economic opportunities.

JB: Do you think that the class system, particularly here in your adopted country of Britain, is a major barrier that stops people rising out of poverty?

PB: I don't believe that at all. In England, society is one where people are acutely aware of small differences. If a civil servant expects to get a KCB, then gets a CBE, he is mortified. If he expects to get a CBE and gets an OBE, he is again mortified. The perception of differences runs across society. If you look into pubs you have a lounge bar, a saloon bar and a public bar, frequented by slightly different people. But these differences are not the same thing as barriers. John Major, when he became leader of the Conservative Party, said he would work towards the elimination of a class system. I don't know what he meant by that. Did he think everyone would drink gin and tonic, which is the upper-class drink? Or should they try dry sherry, which is also upper-class, instead of drinking sweet sherry or port, which the lower class drinks? John Major himself is the son of a variety artist. His predecessor was the daughter of a grocer. Her predecessor was the son of a small builder. Not far back, we have Ramsay MacDonald, who was an illegitimate son of a fisherwoman. England is an open society, whose differences are not barriers.

JB: Let me turn to another area where critics are ranged against you. Many people claim poverty in less developed parts of the world is the result of huge population pressures. How do you react to that?

PB: I simply say it is not true. It varies because you find some of the poorest and most backward countries are very thinly populated. In much of Africa, land – including, for example, the former Congo, now Zaïre (it has a different name now) – is so thinly populated over a large area, land is a free good. And on the contrary, some of the most densely populated countries are very prosperous. Take Hong Kong and Singapore.

JB: So these people that get behind these demands for population control, you think are completely misguided?

PB: They are misguided, although they are often guided by self-interest.

JB: Why is that? How is that?

PB: They benefit from suggestions that they should control people's lives.

JB: Peter, how did you come to get interested in the economics of developing countries?

PB: Because years ago, long before them, I did a study on the rubber industry, and then one on West Africa. That then gradually led me to apply this field of so-called development economics. By these specific studies was started my interest in the subject.

JB: Who or what most influenced you in those early days into doing those particular studies, which in turn led to the broader interest?

PB: I should say I was influenced for a while by a man called John Jewkes, Stanley Dennison, and soon by Basil Yamey – he influenced me more than anyone else. Dennison was a senior undergraduate at Cambridge when I was a freshman. He took some interest in me, and started coaching me. Jewkes wrote on a number of subjects which interested me, but neither of them were professors of mine.

JB: And later, when you came to the LSE, you met Basil Yamey, and he was a great co-author of yours.

PB: Yes, yes.

JB: Let's talk for a moment about Basil. He was of course your co-author of a number of your reports. You were close colleagues at the London School of Economics. You co-wrote at least a couple of books together, I believe.

PB: The reason we worked personally, but professionally also, so well was that he has a much sharper mind than I have. I was a more restless mind, as someone who had to look into it. He had a much sharper mind than I have. These are complements; we complement each other.

JB: When did you meet?

PB: I think in 1947, at the LSE.

JB: Was he already a market-oriented economist?

PB: Very market-oriented, yes.

JB: And you played off each other? There were synergies there?

PB: Yes. What happened is, I had to do a study of West African trade, which was originally commissioned by the then Colonial Office, and I couldn't quite assemble a great deal of material. On the whole, I think, it turned out rather successful. I was not very good putting it together, and I thought of asking R.H. Coase to help me with it. Coase couldn't because he was on the point of going to America, and he suggested I try Basil Yamey, and it worked.

JB: So it was Coase that introduced you to Yamey?

PB: Very largely, yes.

JB: I was reading the other day *The Oxford Dictionary of Political Quotations*, and you are credited with the following quote: 'Aid is a process by which the poor in rich countries subsidise the rich in poor countries.' Amplify that a little.

PB: When people talk about aid, they only mean government-to-government subsidies. Aid doesn't go to the miserable creatures you see on your television screen, it goes to the rulers. And the rulers tend to be the most prosperous people in their countries. That is what I meant.

JB: Is money going from the poor taxpayer in rich countries through our government . . .

PB: . . . to the other government, whose personnel tends to be well off, relative to the rest of the population.

JB: So it sounds as if you feel aid can't do all that much to help these countries develop.

PB: No, certainly not. If you want to talk in semi-technical language, the most aid can do, at best, is slightly reduce the cost of borrowing in these countries. These countries can borrow very heavily abroad; both their governments and other private people.

JB: So the very best scenario is it is a slight help. From that, I would take it, it is often a major hindrance.

PB: Yes. It contributes, promotes the politicisation of life in these countries. And that, in turn, intensifies the political struggle and diverts people's attention from productive economic activity to political life.

JB: Because that's where huge amounts of money are to be made.

PB: And it strengthens people's rules over their fellow man.

JB: So what you're saying really is that aid incentivises bad policy.

PB: On the whole, yes.

JB: The more I make a mess of things as a Third World president or prime minister, the more the West pours money into my coffers.

PB: Yes indeed. That is evident in the case of Ethiopia – the misery in Ethiopia, which was freely shown on our television screens, was promoted not by drought but by government policies. The suppression of trade brought it about. The slightly unfavourable weather conditions, leading to belt-tightening, led to the catastrophes.

JB: If you were President of Ethiopia, what would you be doing?

PB: I suspect, like most other people, my first concern would be to keep myself in office. That would be my first concern. If I wanted to promote the welfare of the population at large, quite obviously I would promote peaceful commerce with Western economies, market-oriented countries.

JB: And that's in turn led to the development of a whole sub-discipline of economics called development economics.

PB: Yes.

JB: How much were those early days influenced by the Marshall Plan?

PB: Well, the advocates of foreign aid use the Marshall Plan as an example: 'Look what the Marshall Plan has done.' Well, there was no comparison at all between foreign aid and the Marshall Plan. The economies of western Europe had to be restored, not developed. The economies of the so-called Third World, to use a fashionable cliché, had to be developed. With Marshall aid, West Germany and western Europe had to be restored, not developed. The people of these countries, particularly Germany, had institutions and attitudes appropriate to material progress, as is obvious from their achievement.

JB: I know I have to be very careful with the words I use around you, but let me ask you, why did you just say that 'the Third World' is a cliché?

PB: Because I think it is completely inappropriate to lump together three-quarters of mankind under one category. Until the development of foreign aid, nobody thought of lumping together Asia, Africa and Latin America into one category.

JB: What would you prefer to say?

PB: I would prefer to say Asia, Africa and Latin America.

JB: Let's broaden this out. Why, in your view, do some countries develop whilst others stay stagnant?

PB: Economic performance and progress depend on people's attitudes and the policies of government. It does not depend on natural resources, but it depends on the conduct of people. And not on their numbers, but on their conduct.

JB: Could you amplify that a little? Their commercial conduct?

PB: Well, some people are more interested in improving their material lot than others are. That is so in the so-called Third World as in the West.

JB: How do you react to the accusation that large, rich Western countries have exploited poorer countries, and it is that exploitation that has led them to be in the sorry state that many of them are today?

PB: There is absolutely no truth in it whatsoever. Just look around. Which are the most prosperous countries in Asia and Africa? Those with the most Western contact. Singapore and Hong Kong would be the limiting cases. The poorest and most backward are those with no external contacts, the limiting cases being the Amazonian Indians and tribesfolk in Central Africa.

JB: If colonialisation and exploitation by the West are not the reasons why parts of Africa and Asia and other parts of the world are so poor, what is the explanation?

PB: I would say, a lack of people's ambitions and the conduct of the government.

JB: How can a Third World, less-developed country hope to compete these days with advanced Western economies?

PB: They benefit from the presence of Western economies. They don't have to compete with them. They can take advantage of the presence of advanced Western economies which provide sources of raw materials or industrial goods, and advanced technology. It's like what the open frontier was to America in the early days of western American colonisation.

JB: A hundred years ago, countries such as Argentina, for example, ranked among the wealthiest in the world. Now they struggle to get into the top twenty or thirty. What's happened there?

PB: Government policies. That is quite straightforward. Above all Perón, but others as well – that's easily explained. As I said, material achievement and progress depend on people's attitudes and the conduct of government.

JB: Take today, some of the very poorest Central African countries. Many would say that they cannot possibly take off without substantial investments of aid. You clearly disagree with that.

PB: Look. In the past, a number of African countries, long before aid was invented, developed by the efforts of the people and the conduct of the government. Take for example Ghana, or the Gold Coast as it then was. There are millions of acres of cocoa in Ghana and in Nigeria, incidentally, every acre owned, planted and operated by Africans, which incidentally also shows that the notion that the people of these countries are incapable of taking a long view in economic affairs is manifestly untrue. A cocoa tree takes six years before it yields any crop, and yet these people, hundreds of thousands of them, planted cocoa trees – Africans. And the same applies, incidentally, going to the other side of the world, to South-East Asia. The Malays are supposed to be people living for the day, watching the coconuts fall off the tree. In fact, they also have billions of acres under smallholders' cultivation – in Malaysia and in Indonesia.

JB: Let's talk about some other successes. Hong Kong – you visited Hong Kong. How do you credit its success?

PB: Chinese industry and resourcefulness, British administration and maintenance of law and order.

JB: What other countries do you admire that have managed to . . .

PB: I don't admire, just notice. I try not to judge, but just to describe and analyse.

JB: Which would be your best example of a country that has followed the kind of advice that you'd give, and which would be the worst example?

PB: The best example is Hong Kong.

JB: And the worst?

PB: Any number of African countries – Ethiopia, for example.

JB: Don't countries with very low or even no natural resources face a great disadvantage?

PB: No. Singapore and Hong Kong have no natural resources to speak of. Hong Kong was an empty rock, until the middle of the 19th century. Singapore was swamp, no natural resources. The only resource which matters is human beings, that is the ultimate resource, to use a phrase coined by Julian Simon.

JB: So it is the people and their attributes; and the rules within which they operate.

PB: Yes, but it tends to depend on themselves because the rules under which they operate depend on the government which is brought about or put in place by the people. Property rights are extremely important in securing personal freedom and the rule of law. I have recently been reading a very interesting book on this subject by Richard Pipes, who is a research professor at Harvard. And the book is called *Property and Freedom*. It is not the easiest reading in the world, but it is intelligible if you concentrate. And that elaborates the importance of property and personal freedom. Preoccupation with inequality tends to undermine property rights.

JB: So what you are saying is that differences in income spur envy, and envy leads to an attack on property rights?

PB: Yes, particularly if you call them differences. That is less likely to happen than if you call them inequalities.

JB: When you first began to publish these ideas, to talk about these ideas, how were you received?

PB: I'll give you an unambiguous answer – badly!

JB: By everybody, by your fellow academics, by the public?

PB: No, by my fellow academics, because there were oh so many of them on the gravy train of aid. But from the public at large, I had quite substantial fan mail. They came across my views and replied to me. The theme was generally, of this fan mail, thank you for helping me to keep my sanity.

JB: So it was members of the public who had come to similar conclusions themselves?

PB: Yes, quite often came to similar conclusions, but did not know how to formulate them. I formulated them for them.

JB: Let's talk about the gravy train. The grants they were getting from international agencies or the grants they were getting to go and do studies?

PB: Many of them were on various forms of government contracts, were and are. Development economics and foreign aid are intimately linked. There was no development aid until President Truman's Point Four in 1949. That led to foreign aid and that led to development economics. There was no such subject as development economics, until after the Second World War.

JB: Was anyone else besides you and your co-author, Basil Yamey, doing similar work?

PB: No. The nearest thing were certain anthropologists, like Raymond Firth, for example, who was a professor of anthropology at London.

JB: What was he doing?

PB: He made studies. For example, Malayan fishing villages.

JB: And he was coming to similar conclusions to you?

PB: He did not branch into this, but he gave good descriptions, and analysis of life among the fisher folk of Malaya.

JB: And you as an economist could look at that work and see that the fishermen were acting in a long-term rational way, that they were making long-term investments.

PB: Yes.

JB: Just like your cocoa growers and your rubber growers. Your first scholarly articles were about the pig and milk industries in England and how the government had moved in on them and created so-called marketing boards which effectively had rigged the market.

PB: I published of course to a considerable extent under the pressure from the farmers themselves. Whereas in West Africa, they instantly saw depressed farming incomes.

JB: And in England, they were introduced in peacetime, whereas I think in West Africa they were more of a wartime creation.

PB: Yes. But clearly they can be carried on indefinitely.

JB: So the pig breeders and dairy farmers got together with the government to rig the market to increase prices . . .

PB: Incomes, really.

JB: . . . to stabilise their incomes at higher levels, and this was your first work as a young economist, your first published work.

PB: Yes.

JB: Let's talk about three of your best-known books, and how they came to be written and the impact that they had, in chronological order. *The Rubber Industry*, your first major piece of work – that really came about how? What were the origins of that piece of work?

PB: I worked for a firm of East Indian merchants and rubber growers. That largely influenced me to write that book. And a major theme of that book is the importance of the rubber-growing smallholders which up to that point was not recognised.

JB: And when you returned, you wrote a report for the Colonial Office . . .

PB: Yes.

JB: . . . and then that report was turned into the full-blown . . .

PB: Yes, they were separate. That report, which I have here in this flat, I rather regret it. I was over-stating things over-emphatically and I regret it.

JB: When the full book came out, it began the process of establishing your reputation. It was the first major building block, would I say, in the corpus, the Bauer . . . ?

PB: I should say, possibly, some of my earlier articles, just about the same time. I had an article about the working of rubber regulation in the *Economic Journal* and that created, attracted, a certain amount of attention.

JB: What was the argument of that article?

PB: How the rubber regulation worked. And how unfairly it treated smallholders. And that created a certain amount of attention. The importance of smallholders at all.

JB: The next major piece of work was the book on West African trade. Tell us a little bit about how that came about.

PB: I think the way it came is that there was a lot of agitation, mostly behind the scenes, about the operations in West Africa of the United Africa Company, which is a subsidiary of Unilever, and it was proposed that there should be an inquiry by the Monopolies Commission into the activities of the United Africa Company. Some people in the Colonial Office felt it was not a suitable subject for the Monopolies Commission, it is better to actually investigate the situation and write about it. That's how that book came about.

JB: The big contribution I recollect was that you demonstrated that these small farmers, in whatever industry, whatever particular part of agriculture they might be in, were able to take the long-term view, that they could invest in crops that took a great many years to mature.

PB: Applied both to Malaya and to West Africa.

JB: What was the reception at the time? Because they both came out from reputable publishers. Were they well received, well reviewed?

PB: No. Not at all.

JB: What do you credit that to?

PB: That leads us into the murky field of the sociology of knowledge. You can explain people's views, examine them in terms of logic, empirical evidence, but why people hold certain views is much more difficult and problematical.

JB: When I look at your work, Peter, the third book that stands out to me is your 1961 *Indian Economic Policy* book. Just tell us a little bit about the background of that.

PB: I visited India a bit. I read a good deal about it, and I just wanted to expose some of the shortcomings of the Indian policy.

JB: It was being very much held up as an example, wasn't it? It kept introducing five-year plans.

PB: Yes. Of course, the very idea of five-year plans reflects a Soviet influence, because five-year plans started with Soviet five-year plans.

JB: Looking at the rest of your work, it seems to me it splits into two halves after *The Rubber Industry* book, the *West African Trade* book, and the *Indian Economic Policy* book. You wrote several texts with Basil Yamey, and what I often think of as my favourite Bauer book, *Dissent on Development*, and then you had many books of collections of your articles and speeches that came out.

PB: Not all that many. *Dissent on Development* is that, and there is one called *Reality and Rhetoric*, which came after *Dissent on Development*, which is also a collection of papers. Right now, a book of mine has been published, within the last few days, by Princeton. That is a collection of papers.

JB: Are there, in all these decades of your writing and studying, any so-called Third World countries that you would point to as being good examples? Are there any particular political leaders you admire?

PB: One of the people I admire most is B. R. Shenoy, an Indian economist who figures prominently in some of my writings. I would say, as a polity, I admire Hong Kong. There is a country with no natural resources whatever, and it has become a major industrial power.

JB: We talked before about your work on marketing boards. Some of your early work in your first job as an agricultural economist concerned the marketing boards in the United Kingdom, and in your later work in Ghana, of course, you came across marketing boards there.

PB: You see, in the West, the farmers are a powerful political lobby. And that enables them – obviously, presently, common agricultural policy is the latest phase – to have their incomes maintained at the expense of the taxpayer, or at the expense of the consumer, which is government intervention. In the so-called Third World the situation is exactly the other way around. The urban groups are far more powerful than the farmers. And that is how it has come about in West African marketing boards, which are buying monopolies that manage to keep farm incomes well below world market prices.

JB: So, in the advanced economies, marketing boards enhance incomes of farmers. In Third World countries, they depress their income. Would you say some of your work in the area of development economics, where you put so much emphasis on human capital and human attributes, really is a precursor of many more recent developments in the theory of human capital?

PB: I never used the expression human capital. I think although it is very widely accepted, it is not a fortunate expression. For example, in South-East Asia, particularly Malaysia, the immigrant Chinese (who are not only penniless, who are very, very poor, but also illiterate) can hardly be said to contain much capital, in the accepted sense of the term. They have the right motivation for material progress. I don't like the term human capital. You see, capital is a man-made instrument of production; that is not the case for human beings.

JB: How much of an audience have you enjoyed in countries such as India? How much of your views have been translated and broadcast outside of the British and American markets?

PB: I had a certain following in India. That was because there was an outstanding Indian economist who largely independently of me came to the same conclusion I did.

JB: This is B. R. Shenoy. Tell us a little about Shenoy.

PB: Shenoy was a magnificent man. He was a hero, and he was a saint. I once gave a lecture in his memory in India, and I said I consider it an honour that I should lecture in memory of such a man.

JB: He was highly critical of central government. The five-year plans of the Indians – he foresaw that they would all fail and collapse. Are there disciples of Peter Bauer now out in academia or in the policy world?

PB: No.

JB: Surely someone must have picked up your baton and be writing and publishing on the lines that you were doing.

PB: To some extent, you can say that of Basil Yamey, who is a bit younger than myself, and who I influenced very much (he also influenced me, I might add). There was a Turk called Gonensay who to some extent followed my ideas.

JB: And George Ayittey, maybe?

PB: Yes. I think if you add him you are right.

JB: I seem to recall you speaking favourably of a Canadian, Usher.

PB: Yes indeed. A first-class statistician who exposed the misleading use of statistics in the context of national income statistics. A first-class man.

JB: These are the statistics that show people possibly enjoying low incomes. These tables one sees in development economics books, showing that people in a particular country do not earn enough.

PB: An annual income of forty dollars or so, or thereabouts; and Usher exposed that.

JB: Let's concentrate on that for a moment. How did he expose it? He showed that they didn't take into account ...

PB: Subsistence economy, subsistence production, and various forms of transport costs. That is quite technical.

JB: And essentially, he shows that people simply are not that poor.

PB: Exactly.

JB: They may still be poor, but certainly not as poor as the data.

PB: And Usher was particularly well qualified because he lived for years in Thailand and had a Thai wife.

JB: But today, one does come across the Bauer-type arguments of much more than thirty years ago or so, popping up in journals, think tanks, and the like.

PB: I could claim victory for that. The evident bankruptcy of foreign aid, of development aid, in a number of countries. It has brought people to some extent to their senses.

JB: Have you won the debate?

PB: No. Well, intellectually yes, but not practically. Intellectually I won it. It was not difficult actually.

JB: I can recall you speaking, I think it was in the early 1970s at the Oxford Union, in a debate on population. My recollection is that in that speech you said that the birth of a child depresses average national income, whereas the birth of a pig increases average national income.

PB: That shows the absurdities and the anomalies of conventional wisdom in this field. It is true – not that it matters, the instance

– the birth of a calf or pig adds to national income; the birth of a child immediately depresses it.

JB: And you use this illustration, if my recollection is correct, to illustrate the absurdity of national income statistics.

PB: Yes.

JB: And the absurdity of . . .

PB: The conventional ones.

JB: The conventional ones, and to undermine those who wish to control their population?

PB: Yes. Quite unsuccessfully, I may add.

JB: Given the charitable impulse we all have, how would you advise somebody to direct their personal philanthropy? If somebody came to you who had assets and said they were concerned about a particular Third World country, that was struggling to emerge, what would you advise them to do?

PB: Find out, to locate a person with a real experience in this country. Medical missionaries or missionaries. See how they operate and help them.

JB: You wouldn't advise them to do anything in terms of the underlying institutions of the society?

PB: No, because, you see, there is a great deal of condescension in discussions here in the West towards the so-called Third World. It is implied that we have emerged or developed without external assistance or help, but these blighted people can't. And I don't hold with that.

JB: I know one has to be very careful with one's words around you, Peter. I know one word that you don't like at all is *robber-baron*.

PB: Yes.

JB: What would you say to people who say the early American capitalists in the late 19th and early 20th centuries were robber-barons? What do you say to them?

PB: I would say they were mistaken. They may be well-meaning, but they are mistaken, because the so-called robber-barons were mostly creative entrepreneurs.

JB: Are we back to envy? Is this envy-driven?

PB: In a large measure, yes. Misunderstandings, genuinely. But very largely envy-driven, particularly in England, or the Anglo-Saxon countries. Envy is a very powerful factor in politics.

JB: In your view, these were great men who brought a great deal of wealth, created a great deal of wealth and created jobs, advanced ...

PB: You can think of exceptions of people who were dishonest and so on, but very largely this is the situation. Take for example Henry Ford.

JB: Right.

PB: He pioneered the mass-produced automobile that really transformed existence.

JB: Let's turn away from those early books and talk in more general terms about how you came to be broadly defined as a market-oriented economist. Who most influenced the development of your thinking?

PB: To some extent, Hayek. But to a large extent, I developed it myself. For instance, when I was an undergraduate in the mid-thirties in Cambridge, economics students, the whole economics faculty, were all admirers of the Soviet system. I was critical from the word go, because I say a society which had only one employer cannot be a free society. But I developed this myself.

JB: When would you have met Hayek? When did you first come across him?

PB: For a short time, at the LSE. When I first came. I was at the LSE two different spells. My first spell he was there, just briefly, and I met him there. But I was also, of course, influenced, like thousands of other people, by his book *The Road to Serfdom*.

JB: What of his earlier works would you have read?

PB: Some of his essays. 'The Use of Knowledge in Society', I think, is an extremely important work.

JB: And how important a figure would you judge Hayek to have been, in the broad context of the 20th century?

PB: I would say he is one of the intellectual giants.

JB: And his founding of the Mont Pélerin society. How important was that? To network the remnant of classical liberal scholars.

PB: In the early days, the mid to late forties, I think it was very important to help a very good field, so they could know they were not entirely alone – that there were others that thought like they did. By now, these ideas have been so widely accepted. I don't think its significance is what it used to be.

JB: Your name in German, the name Bauer means . . .

PB: Peasant.

JB: Peasant. And when you were elevated to the House of Lords by Queen Elizabeth II, I believe you joked about British society being in your view classless. You said in your case you'd gone from peasant to peer in one generation.

PB: In one lifetime.

JB: In one lifetime. Slightly more than one generation, true. So from peasant to peer in one lifetime.

PB: Yes.

JB: What can we learn from that example? What does that example tell us?

PB: Yet another countless example that England is an open society.

JB: How significant has it been for you, being a member of the House of Lords?

PB: Needless to say, I am extremely glad to be there. My influence has been absolutely negligible and, by and large, I have been disappointed by the level of discourse in the House of Lords. All of us there have security of tenure. In fact, the opinions you hear are the conventional opinions of the so-called quality dailies.

JB: Tell me about Milton Friedman. His life and yours have overlapped at times.

PB: He took a sabbatical in England and he chose membership of my college, and I learned a great deal from Milton Friedman.

JB: This is 1953–4, I believe?

PB: Yes.

JB: So you were professional colleagues together there for a year.

PB: Yes, yes.

JB: What was that like? You were both young men.

PB: He was a bit older than I am, but he instantly made the rank: he was superior.

JB: I am just trying to imagine what it must have been like at Caius in 1953–4. You would have been 37, 38, 39 years old. Milton and Rose Friedman would have been maybe four or five years older than you. There must have been intellectual sparks flying around the pair of you, with your views and Caius in the fifties. Surely in the common room there must have been ferocious debates?

PB: No. Debates, discussions, at Caius on the whole, as at many other colleges, were very disappointing. The things we discussed were: should staircases be numbered by letter or by number, that sort of thing. Now there was actually one outstanding figure at the time at Caius; there were actually several good ones. One outstanding figure, R.A. Fisher, who was a giant, one of the makers of modern statistics, and also almost certainly the greatest British biologist since Darwin, and he and Friedman were on the whole on the same wavelength, and they talked together.

JB: What were the two sharpest minds you ever came across?

PB: I should say – this is not such an easy answer – but I would say Milton Friedman and Basil Yamey.

JB: What makes you say that?

PB: Because I knew them and I read their writings. And, as it were,

I knew both of them personally.

JB: You are always very precise in your use of terms. And for all that I've been a student of yours for thirty years, you still correct me. And I believe that this is on your coat of arms ... what is your motto?

PB: Let us be free from cant.

JB: Let us be free from cant.

PB: Cant, yes.

JB: What do you hope that the scholars of the future will say when they look back at your life and your work and the body of work that you achieved? What do you think they will say about this lone voice raised against the establishment?

PB: Perhaps some may say I was a man of moral courage, which is seriously lacking in the contemporary scene. Certainly, I will not have a standing in the eyes of the world such as Buchanan has, for instance, or Hayek, but I think I shall be commended by some people for clarity and courage.

## 2 THE MILTON FRIEDMAN PRIZE FOR ADVANCING LIBERTY

## The Milton Friedman Prize

On Thursday, 9 May 2002, Peter Bauer was due to be recognised at the 25th Anniversary Dinner of the Cato Institute in Washington, DC, as the first-ever winner of the $500,000 Milton Friedman Prize for Advancing Liberty.

Unfortunately, Peter passed away on 2 May. However, he had been planning to attend and had written his acceptance speech. In the circumstances John Blundell, a judge who had already been asked to speak on the selection of Peter, gave not only his own speech but also the acceptance. Both are reproduced below.

On the stage at the dinner with Blundell was 1967 Nobel Laureate in Economics Milton Friedman and the Glass Prize Sculpture. Peter's executors asked that, as he had no family, the sculpture and certificate (also read out by Blundell) be put on permanent display at the Cato Institute.

## The achievements of Peter Bauer
*John Blundell*

I first met Peter Bauer in the fall of 1971 when I was a freshman at the London School of Economics. The tutor assigned to me was slightly to the left of the Labour Party, which made him a moderate man for that time and place. He suggested at our first meeting that I write a paper for him on a topic of my own choosing so he could begin to get the measure of me. I replied, 'Well, how about something on the Economics of Development and the Third World?' and he seemed very pleased. A week later I handed in a paper entitled 'Trade Not Aid'. 'Oh dear,' he said. 'I'd better give you to Peter Bauer.' Peter's first advice to me was 'Don't read Hayek or Mises until you are a graduate student. As an undergraduate they will only get you into trouble.' Well, Peter was spot-on. But he was too late . . . and I'm still getting in trouble.

His second advice was to study history and I recall Elton's *The Practice of History* being thrust into my hands. Without history we cannot understand society. Without history we cannot value and we certainly cannot reclaim liberty.

Thirdly he opened the eyes of a very narrow economist to the importance of an interdisciplinary approach to understanding society and to promoting liberty. But as well as being a great scholar and tutor Peter was also a man of great physical and moral courage, as he showed during the deadly student riots of the late 1960s when he publicly and boldly and repeatedly stood by his principles. He refused to let the left tyrannise him. He refused to let the left cow him.

So why did we, the nine judges, select Peter Bauer?

It was Peter who, after years of study of private enterprise in Africa and Asia, proved that the poor are *held back* by central planning, *held back* by large-scale state investment and *held back* by foreign aid.

It was Peter who showed that the solutions proposed by all other development economists were not solutions at all – nor were they even neutral. Rather they were positively harmful.

It was Peter who in the scholarly literature changed how we see the world within his meticulous analysis of markets and migration, population and price controls, investment and so-called commodity stabilisation schemes.

It was Peter who cautioned us not to use a warm, fuzzy word like 'aid' but rather the more accurate 'government-to-government transfers'.

It was Peter who taught that aid is the process by which the *poor* in *rich* countries subsidise the *rich* in *poor* countries.

It was Peter who showed us that peasants in poor countries routinely invest in crops which do not bear fruit for six years! That is, the poor peasant takes a longer view than most politicians.

It was Peter who conjectured that aid politicised and corrupted recipient countries, drawing talent into government that would otherwise have remained in the productive private sector.

It was Peter who exposed how aid reinforced unsound domestic policies ... to say nothing of repression and the expulsion of productive minorities.

It was Peter who, with Hayek and Mises, prophesied that the Soviet Union could not survive in the long term.

It was Peter who pointed out that in the Third World the primary aim of governments is to stay in power – and aid fuels this.

It was Peter who instructed us not to use the loaded term 'inequalities' but rather 'differences'.

It was Peter who opened our eyes when he commented how strange it was that the birth of a calf represents an increase in GNP and the birth of a child represents a decrease.

It was Peter who convinced us all that aid does not go to the miserable creatures we see on our television screens but rather to their rulers or, should I say, oppressors.

Finally, it was Peter who by personal example showed that, however much you are mocked and execrated, however shell-shocked you may be, you must continue to pursue the truth. And remember that when Peter started 'all', I repeat 'all', other development economists favoured 'central planning as the *first* condition of progress'.

Alas, Peter is no longer with us in person. But his courage and his teachings remain as an imperishable example to us and to future generations.

Two years ago I made a video of Peter with the Liberty Fund of Indianapolis, Indiana, and my last question to him was, 'How will history judge you?' He replied, 'I will not have the standing of a Hayek but I think I shall be commended by some people for clarity and courage.'

Well, Peter, there are rather a lot of people here tonight to commend you, above all others, as the first winner of the Milton Friedman Prize for Advancing Liberty.

Had Peter been able to be with us, I would now be presenting to him his certificate. Let me read it to you. It says:

*The Milton Friedman Prize for Advancing Liberty 2002.*
Peter Bauer
In recognition of his tireless and pioneering scholarly
contributions to understanding the role of property and
free markets in wealth creation, his demonstration of
the negative effects on poor nations of government-to-
government transfers, and his inspiring vision of a world of
free and prosperous people.
Awarded this 9th day of May 2002

I spoke to Peter the day after he got the news of his prize, about a month ago now, and he'd already written his acceptance speech, which I will read in a moment. But I want to convey to you a feeling of how pleased he was. I think to win a prize from Cato, his favourite think tank, would have been very special to him, and to win a prize named after Milton Friedman would also have been very special. But to win *the* Milton Friedman prize from *the* Cato Institute was almost beyond belief for him. So let me just conclude by reading to you the sixty or seventy words he penned and planned to deliver this evening:

I'm much gratified by the Milton Friedman Prize from the Cato Institute. Cato and Milton Friedman have influenced the climate of opinion by heroically defending and encouraging the principles of limited government, personal liberty and self-reliance. It is also important for me to add that Milton Friedman has been my mentor over many years. Cato as an institution and Milton Friedman as an individual scholar have genuine influence. Certainly, they've influenced me. I want to thank Cato and Milton Friedman.

## 3 THE SAYER OF TRUTH: A PERSONAL TRIBUTE TO PETER BAUER
*James M. Buchanan*[1]

Objectively considered, and apart from a long-standing personal friendship, Peter Bauer had a formative influence on my own career. Almost single-handedly he orchestrated my academic year at Cambridge University in 1961–2. In 1960 or thereabouts, when Peter was just leaving Cambridge for the London School of Economics, he realised that there was an open slot for the public finance lectures after Alan Prest's departure. Peter encouraged me to, first, express an interest and, second, to accept the invitation once offered. Meanwhile, he somehow accomplished the more difficult task of getting the university to invite me – a neophyte from the boondocks of American academia. And life among the tribes in Cambridge opened my eyes to the sometimes idealised world of high-table talk and Oxbridge snobbery. But to be a guest of Sir Dennis Robertson at a Trinity College feast, and to see James Meade at his best, and Joan Robinson at her worst – these were experiences to be treasured, the latter made all the more surprising when I learned from Peter that he had been Joan's assistant for two years while he was a student.

During my three separate stints at LSE, all in the 1960s, Peter and Basil Yamey, Peter's co-author, were my best friends, both in the common room and in the social setting outside the academic

1   This essay was originally written for *Public Choice* and is reproduced by kind permission of the editor of that journal.

halls. Over many meals, at the Bauer, Buchanan or Yamey estab-
lishments, we resolved most issues of the world and subjected
our economist peers to the criticism they really did deserve. And
shopping with Peter Bauer, a man of impeccable taste, among the
London antique shops for just the proper small piece of furniture
was, for me, an entry to a culture to which I could only aspire,
never achieve. At times, however, Peter did not quite seem to fit
the niche that he wanted to occupy, as for instance at the Hurl-
ingham Club, an establishment that appeared a bit more sporting
than Peter, even at his best.

Peter Bauer was among the very first, if not the first, distinguished lecturers that Warren Nutter and I invited to the University of Virginia after we set up the Thomas Jefferson Center for
Studies in Political Economy and Social Philosophy, the Center
that was to become notorious in the ideologically charged atmos-
phere of the early cold war years. Peter later become a regular visitor, in Charlottesville, Blacksburg and Fairfax, whenever possible,
on his increasingly frequent trips to America in the 1970s, 1980s
and 1990s.

He valued good things, including food and drink. He paid my
wife, Ann, a fine natural cook, the supreme compliment when he
remarked 'the cooking is good in this house'. I can hear his voice
now with those words, and I often suggested to Ann that she
should write a cookbook under that very title.

Peter Bauer was, first of all, a simple economist, who valued
honesty above all else. I do not use the word 'simple' here lightly or
provocatively. To Peter Bauer, economics is a simple subject, with
relatively few basic principles. What is required is straightforward
honesty in applying these principles to the problems confronted
in the real world. His ability and his willingness to cut through

the complex cant of modern economics did not serve him well in the disciplinary popularity contests. In one sense, Peter Bauer was a direct follower of Adam Smith, both in his understanding that incentives affect behaviour and in his willingness to extend the rationality postulate to include the peasant farmers as well as the traders, and, importantly, the bureaucrats. In a very real way, public choice, as a research programme, was embodied naturally in Bauer's analyses of the politicised development schemes of mid-century. He despised the charlatans in the temple and took it on himself to expose them at each and every opportunity. Who, among those who knew Peter Bauer, will not recall his clippings from the press, reflecting the absurdities of economic discourse? Somehow or other, Peter seemed to think that such absurdities could not ultimately win the day, or, at least, he was unwilling to resign himself to this prospect. But perhaps there is less honour among the idea merchants than Peter recognised. He may have failed to understand that far too many of his peers in the academy place little or no value on truth, as such. He was not naive, however, in his approach to what truth is and the process of discovery. Indeed, it was Peter Bauer who specifically suggested that I read David Stove as an antidote to the simplistic Popperian dominance in economists' methodology.

Peter Bauer felt that he had a moral obligation to expose the lies being told by his peers. And while he surely did feel that his own ideas were vindicated by the turns of history, he remained pessimistic about prospects for a viable liberal order. The liars are always with us, and neither the events of history nor the triumph of ideas will hold off those who would subvert the truth, which, in political economy, must be continually defended. Such truth has indeed lost a champion.

# 4 PETER BAUER AND THE OBSERVATION OF ECONOMIC LIFE
*Meghnad Desai*

Peter Bauer was unique among economists in one significant way. Economists in the 20th century used a priori, desktop thinking much more than actual observation of economic life. As the subject became specialised, economists, even applied economists, cut themselves off from daily economic life and stuck to published statistics or mathematical models. Those who actually described economic reality got shunted off to anthropology or geography or business studies.

Peter was one economist in the 'Anglo-Saxon' tradition who stuck to direct observation as a major mode of analysis. His studies of West African trade and Malayan rubber plantations are valuable because they are informed by direct observation. You can sense the active participation of Peter in the reality he is observing. The carefully observed detail makes his studies special. But there is more than just direct observation. His studies are also imbued with robust theory. This is not formal mathematical theory in the neo-classical fashion. He is more in the classical Smithian tradition. People engage in the daily activity of earning a livelihood. In the course of that activity they respond to signals, they innovate, they enter into association. They economise.

The people in the Bauer world are not victims. They are not irrational nor do they suffer from what the imperial imagination called the peasant mentality of limited wants, reluctance to work, being lazy or shiftless. They are not different from any other people because they are black Africans or brown Indians or Malays. Like people anywhere they respond to price signals and make themselves better off if they can. They are not rational maximisers of the neo-classical textbooks. Implicitly they live in a social background, but that is not an obstacle.

In such a Smithian world, there can be problems caused by government interference. Peter's work arose out of the problems created by colonial development policies. These policies were driven by a desire to do good, to help the helpless colonised victim, to assuage imperial guilt. Principal among these policies were price stabilisation schemes which tried to reduce the price received by farmers in good times and to raise it in bad times. This, of course, meant that the signalling properties of prices were no longer effective. Unfortunately, but predictably, these policies ended up harming rather than helping activity. The principal reason for this unintended but not unpredictable outcome was that these 'friends of the people' did not trust the people to know what was good for them. They also took the rather peculiar view that the theory which worked at home did not work in the outbacks. Thus the colonised poor were different from their masters in not being able to know their own interests and in not being subject to the same economic logic. Sadly, this peculiar set of beliefs was held by people who thought they were being anti-racists in thinking the way they did.

It was against those kinds of policies, meant to do good but harmful in the final instance, that Peter Bauer began his crusade in the 1950s. His mode of thinking was as unfashionable as was the content of his polemic. This is what caused much confusion, even among those economists who thought of themselves as conservative defenders of the market. Peter was not a conservative free marketeer nor a neo-classical thinker. He came from another tradition in economics. He was a classical Smithian.

The classical Smithian thinker asserts the basic sameness of all people as being able to comprehend their own self-interest. He also believes that the driving force of self-interest in pursuit of well-being is of universal application. He is not a relativist but an absolute universalist. In Peter Bauer's case this absolute universalism was reinforced by direct observation rather than a priori thinking. His studies of West Africa and Malaya were powerful because of this combination of ideas and observation. In West Africa they failed to have the sort of impact they should have had. Africa has, even now, not grasped the simple lessons of how to let the market economy work by itself. In Malaysia, eventually, market-led policies were followed. Despite some false starts Malaysia, like much of East Asia, instituted government policies which did not cut against the grain of the market.

In India, where Peter spent much time engaging in polemical combat in the late 1950s and 1960s, he had less success. Here he did not have the time to undertake any of the well-observed microeconomic studies he had conducted in Africa and South-East Asia. His message was also distorted by the stupidities of cold war propaganda, of which he was involuntarily made a part. But his instincts were sure. It took 40 years before India changed its ways. It boasted a large entrepreneurial class, honed in the hundred years since the first beginnings of modern industry in the 1850s. But following independence, the government of India turned its back on that past, subdued and debilitated the class of entrepreneurs in search of self-sufficiency. Criticisms of economists like Bauer and Schultz were ignored. It took a severe crisis of foreign debt to bring

India back onto a sensible path. Even now, however, the lessons are only reluctantly imbibed.

But in the field of development economics Peter Bauer has come to be recognised as a pioneer because his ideas have won the respect of time. But his methods of study, of close and sympathetic observation without imposing alien values, have yet to win popularity. There are even now too many field studies where investigators go around looking for the workings of neo-classical theories or sniffing around for market failures. A people-oriented, sharply observed economics of development may yet emerge to pay Peter Bauer his ultimate tribute. Let us at least hope so.

# 5 P. T. BAUER'S LEGACY OF LIBERTY
*James A. Dorn*

Peter Bauer was a friend and mentor. I first began working with Peter in 1985, when I was organising a conference in his honour, which the Cato Institute held in Washington on 1 May 1986. From the very beginning, I could see his intensity, his clarity of thought, and his passion for individual freedom and limited government, as well as his great intellectual depth and curiosity. That conference resulted in a special edition of the *Cato Journal* – 'Development Economics after 40 Years: Essays in Honor of Peter Bauer' – and included his famous essay 'The Disregard of Reality', which was later reprinted in *Cato's Letters*.

In September 1990, Peter spoke at Cato's Moscow conference, 'Transition to Freedom: The New Soviet Challenge', where he discussed 'Western Subsidies and Eastern Reform', and argued that market liberalisation, not external aid, would be the key to successful reform. That paper appeared in the *Cato Journal* and in a Russian edition of the conference volume. In 1992, I invited Peter to participate in Cato's Distinguished Lecturer series. His lecture, 'Subsistence, Trade, and Exchange: Understanding Developing Economies', was given on 14 October, at the Watterston House. Two years later, he gave a second lecture at Cato entitled 'Population Explosion: Disaster or Blessing?' Both lectures were published by Cato.

By the mid-1990s, Bauer's work was receiving increasing attention, especially as his market-liberal vision was being vindicated by the collapse of the Soviet Union and by the failure of development aid. To further spread his ideas, I decided to gather some of his key essays, as well as essays by leading economists who had been influenced by his work – such as Karl Brunner, Deepak Lal, Julian Simon, Douglass C. North, Paul Craig Roberts and Alvin Rabushka – and bring out a book, *The Revolution in Development Economics*. That book, co-edited with Steve Hanke and Alan Walters, appeared in 1998. It was later translated into Chinese and published in Shanghai. Peter's final book, *From Subsistence to Exchange and Other Essays*, appeared in 2000. Princeton University Press brought out a special edition as a Cato Institute Book. We were honoured to be a part of that final work.

My happiest moment for Peter was when I learned that he would be the first recipient of the Milton Friedman Prize for Advancing Liberty, which he was to receive at the Cato Institute's 25th Anniversary Dinner in Washington on 9 May 2002. The *Wall Street Journal* announced the $500,000 prize on 18 April, in an editorial, and Peter received congratulatory letters from around the world. In the last days of his life, before he passed away on 2 May, Peter was in high spirits. As his neighbour revealed:

> Those of us who mourn Peter's passing are nonetheless immensely grateful for the timing of Peter's receipt of the Milton Friedman Prize. It brought great joy to the last few weeks of his life. Furthermore, it provoked such a revival of his spirit and sparkle that most of us forgot the frail state of his health.

All of us at Cato will miss this great man and friend of freedom. His legacy of liberty will be kept alive by his works and by all those individuals he has influenced throughout his long and distinguished career. A brief review of some of his key contributions follows.

During the 1950s and 1960s, Bauer fought almost alone against the rising tide of state-led development policy. It was not unusual at the time to hear well-known economists advocate socialism as the answer to poverty. In 1957, Stanford University economist Paul A. Baran wrote, 'The establishment of a socialist planned economy is an essential, indeed indispensable, condition for the attainment of economic and social progress in underdeveloped countries.'

Bauer sought to convince the so-called development experts that their theories and policies were inconsistent with sound economic reasoning and with reality. His message was loud and clear: comprehensive central planning, foreign aid, price controls and protectionism perpetuate poverty rather than eliminate it; the growth of government intervention politicises economic life and reduces individual freedom.

The failure of development planning – as revealed most notably in the collapse of the Soviet regime, the ongoing transition from plan to market in China, and the dismal record of foreign aid in Africa and India – has led to a revolution in thinking about the determinants of economic advance. Even the World Bank, in its 1997 *World Development Report*, admitted that the notion that 'good advisers and technical experts would formulate good policies, which good governments would then implement for the good of society' was naive. 'Governments embarked on fanciful schemes. Private investors, lacking confidence in public policies or in the steadfastness of leaders, held back. Powerful rulers acted arbitrarily. Corruption became endemic. Development faltered, and poverty endured.' Exactly as Bauer had predicted.

For Bauer, the essence of development is the expansion of individual choices, and the role of the state is to protect life, liberty and property so that individuals can pursue their own goals and desires. Limited government, not central planning, was his mantra.

Accordingly, in 1957 Bauer wrote in *Economic Analysis and Policy in Underdeveloped Countries*:

> I regard the extension of the range of choice, that is, an increase in the range of effective alternatives open to people, as the principal objective and criterion of economic development; and I judge a measure principally by its probable effects on the range of alternatives open to individuals ... The acceptance of this objective means that I attach significance, meaning, and value to individual acts of choice and valuation, including the individual time preference between the present and the future.

He went on to say that 'my position is much influenced by my dislike of policies or measures which are likely to increase man's power over man; that is, to increase the control of groups or individuals over their fellow men'.

Bauer placed himself firmly in the tradition of the great classical liberals. His adherence to the principles of free trade and free people reflected his deep respect for the dignity, rationality and capabilities of poor people around the world versus the patronising undertones of the development experts who made up 'the spurious consensus'.

In his many articles and books, including *Dissent on Development* (1972), Bauer overturned many of the commonly held beliefs of development economics. He refuted the idea that poverty is self-perpetuating and showed that central planning and large-scale public investment are not preconditions for growth. In his clever fashion he noted, 'It is more meaningful to say that capital is created in the process of development, rather than that development is a function of capital.'

He criticised the idea that poor people could not and would not save for the future, or that they had no motivation to improve their condition. He opposed 'compulsory saving', which he preferred to call 'special taxation', and, like modern supply-side economists, recognised the detrimental effects of high taxes on economic activity. Bauer also saw that government-directed investment funded by 'special taxation' would increase 'inequality in the distribution of power'.

Unlike many development experts, Bauer did not see the poor as 'lifeless bricks, to be moved about by some master builder'. Rather, his experience in Malaya (now Malaysia), in the late 1940s, and in West Africa led him to recognise the importance of individual effort on the part of small landowners and traders in moving from subsistence to a higher standard of living. As he wrote in *The Development Frontier* (1991):

> A developed infrastructure was not a precondition for the emergence of the major cash crops of Southeast Asia and West Africa. As has often been the case elsewhere, the facilities known as infrastructure were developed as the economy expanded ... What happened was in very large measure the result of the individual voluntary responses of millions of people to emerging or expanding opportunities created largely by external contacts and brought to their notice in a variety of ways, primarily through the operation of the market. These developments were made possible by firm but limited government, without large expenditures of public funds and without the receipt of large external subventions.

Bauer was perhaps the first economist to recognise the importance of the informal sector and advocated the 'dynamic gains' from international trade – that is, the net gains that result from exposure to new ideas, new methods of production, new products, and new people, or what we would call 'globalisation'. He demonstrated that trade barriers and restrictive immigration and population policies deprive countries of those gains.

For Bauer government-to-government aid was neither necessary nor sufficient for development, and might actually hinder it. 'To have money is the result of economic achievement, not its precondition,' he argued. Trade, not aid, promotes long-run prosperity. The danger of aid, according to Bauer, is that it increases the power of government, leads to corruption, misallocates resources, and erodes civil society.

Bauer's legacy is a better understanding of the forces that shape economic development, especially the institutions of private property, stable money, free trade, and limited government under a rule of law, which underpin the spontaneous market order. Governments everywhere can learn from his wisdom. Along with Hayek and Friedman, Lord Bauer will be remembered as one of the 20th century's greatest liberals. That is a legacy he can be proud of.

## 6 PETER BAUER IN THE HOUSE OF LORDS
*Ralph Harris*

Peter Bauer's elevation to the House of Lords in 1983 was a welcome signal to the less conformist academic community that even the advocacy of uncompromising views on public policy need not prove a barrier to political preferment.

But he was at once faced with an unexpected dilemma. Since he was included in the government's list of working peers, rather than in the biennial New Year or Birthday Honours, he was required to sign up to supporting the Conservative programme in the division lobby. I remember him afterwards telling me gleefully how, when he complied, he pointed out to Margaret Thatcher that once he was gazetted as a life peer he could vote as he wished!

However, like me, he was never quite at home addressing their Lordships. For academics especially, the voluntary time limit of ten minutes on backbench speeches prevents the full deployment of analysis and evidence. It requires much more careful composition than a relaxed ad lib delivery over half an hour or so, let alone the customary 50 minutes of a university lecture. Accordingly, after making some 20 speeches, he announced that he had earned his peerage and turned up at the House only to meet friends or to vote on rare issues about which he felt particularly strongly. He made one of the shortest interventions I have ever heard when he solemnly rose to announce in four terse sentences his opposition to the War Crimes Bill: 'My Lords, I am of Jewish extraction. My father was killed by the Nazis. I emphatically support the amendment. This bill is another step towards the erosion of the rule of law.' (Though he voted with the majority against the Government's bill, it was finally passed in 1991 over the Lords' 'veto'.)

For me his maiden speech was particularly memorable. It was delivered on 29 June 1983 in the four-day debate on the Queen's Speech, which sets out the new government's programme for the coming year. He naturally selected the day devoted to 'economic and industrial affairs', but with a characteristic show of independence chose to lecture the House on the folly of the welfare state. First came a nod at the convention whereby the 'maiden' puts on a gracious show of modesty. Thus he asked for special indulgence for the reason that 'is all too audible, despite all my efforts to master the language'. Expressing 'awe' for the occasion, he quoted a guest of Louis XIV who, on his first visit to Versailles, was asked what amazed him most. The visitor replied: 'That I should be here.' Yet, he quickly added, perhaps it was not so amazing to find himself in the Lords since the presence of other Hungarians (his old antagonists, Kaldor and Balogh) was simply proof that 'Britain is an open society, as it has been for centuries'.

He then put aside the pleasantries and turned to the government's expressed 'commitment to the welfare state'. This provided the occasion for him to launch into a declaration of war – on his own party! They had won the recent election 'on a wet programme in the hands of a dry prime minister'. It was the old, old story of 'Tory men and Whig measures'. Peers who did not know him must have been startled to hear him embark on his main theme that, in his judgement, speaking as an economist, the fundamental issue of the welfare state was not economic at all, but moral. It was nothing less than 'the responsibility of people to manage their own affairs'.

Were not old age, ill health, raising children, housing and interruption of earnings simply everyday contingencies of life? he asked. His answer: 'Except perhaps for a small and dwindling minority of the poor', responsible people should normally be able to pay for them from savings – as for holidays – or by insurance – 'as they prudently do for the potentially crippling losses of fire or burglary'. Allowing for heavy taxation on the poor – commonly amounting throughout western Europe to about one-fifth of the incomes of the poorest fifth of the population – Lord Bauer announced that the welfare state does not so much redistribute income as 'redistribute responsibility between the agents of the state and private persons'. After all, the social services already claimed 50 per cent of government spending and not far short of 30 per cent of the national income.

He pointed to the distinction between adults who manage their incomes and children who receive pocket money, before observing that: 'The operation of the welfare state tends to reduce the status of adults to that of children.' It further undermines the cohesion of the family which, along with voluntary societies, used to be a source of support in adversity, leaving the state to act as a safety net of last resort. 'The debate ought to be about the individual's and family's responsibility for their own affairs.' Of course, he conceded, there were serious economic effects of the welfare state, but they simply reinforced his general argument. Thus private saving and insurance were obviously undermined by inflation, while high taxes on low incomes reduced the incentive to work. Both evils should be tackled by giving higher priority to reducing taxes. His verdict on both was: 'By politicising life, they create friction, encourage conflict and undermine democratic cohesion.'

In a final challenge to the Tory government that had put him in the Lords and which had just won a landslide victory at the 1983 general election, our professor offered a magisterial warning. If they continued wedded to an expanding welfare state, it could be said of them, as Livy said of Hannibal when Rome was for the taking: 'You know how to gain victories but not how to use them.'

His concluding sentences are worth quoting in full as a mixture of grace and disfavour. 'To be a Member of your Lordships' House is a rare privilege. I believe that the independence it confers imposes an obligation, perhaps even in a maiden speech, to question consensus views which have not always served us well. This belief has informed my speech, which may have been a little controversial, but I hope it was not provocative.' It may have been my imagination, but I thought the customary chorus of 'hear, hear' when a maiden sits down was just a little less than full-throated!

## 7    A DISSIDENT VINDICATED[1]
### *Deepak Lal*

This book collects some of Peter Bauer's recent essays, and
has a handsome and well-deserved appreciation of them in an
introduction by Amartya Sen, the Nobel laureate. The main
characteristics of Lord Bauer's work are best summed up in his
bon mot in the essay entitled 'Disregard of Reality', when discussing the conversion of contemporary economics into a branch of
applied mathematics. He writes: 'What we see is an inversion of
the familiar Hans Andersen story of the Emperor's New Clothes.
Here there are new clothes, and at times they are *haute couture.* But
all too often there is no Emperor within.' In these essays – as in
his past work – he excoriates one fashionable nostrum after the
other: 'vicious circles of poverty', natural resources as a source
of wealth, population growth as a cause of poverty in the Third
World, foreign aid as necessary for development, the purported
role of education in development, the legitimising of envy by the
Christian Churches, the purported destructive effects of Britain's
class society on its economic performance, and the unthinking acceptance of the case for egalitarianism. In each case, with forensic
precision and in stylish prose, he shows that, despite attempts by

1    Professor Lal's review of this collection of essays by Peter Bauer (*From Subsistence
     to Exchange and Other Essays*, Princeton University Press, 2000) was first pub-
     lished in the *Times Literary Supplement* on 15 December 2000. It is reproduced by
     kind permission of the *TLS*.

the best and the brightest to provide rational clothing for these ideas, there is no emperor within.

Bauer has not been merely a critic of the loose thinking of his peers; he also did seminal early work in colonial Malaysia and West Africa on the transition of a subsistence economy to an exchange economy – the title of the lead essay in the book. In this transition, the unsung heroes, as Bauer documented in his closely observed writings on these countries, are the traders – big and small – who have effected the transformation, pioneers of what came to be called the economics of the 'informal sector'. The energy and creativity of this sector are not captured by official statistics, nor is its immense amount of capital formation – as has been recently documented by Hernando de Soto and his collaborators in Peru and Egypt.

But, for a long period, Bauer was virtually a pariah in his chosen sub-discipline – development economics. The fashionable planning and dirigisme of the 1950s and 1960s, based on the priceless economics he castigated, were incompatible with his insistence on the relevance of standard microeconomics and monetary economics to the problems of developing countries. This professional neglect was a tragedy, not only for Bauer, but for the profession. Because of his dissident status, he was not able to obtain the resources to conduct the research based on close observation which his early work had shown to be his forte. However, events have subsequently vindicated almost every dissident position he had taken. As Professor Sen rightly observes in his introduction: 'Like the old lady who went to see *Hamlet* and felt it was full of quotations, a young reader of Bauer's early books may find his arguments rather familiar.' The ideas he is associated with are no longer those of a maverick but very much in the mainstream.

Among the few other notable economists who stuck to the true last of their profession was B. R. Shenoy of Gujarat University. He was the sole eminent Indian economist to issue a note of dissent on the framework of the Indian Second Five Year Plan. This instituted that system of planning and the permit raj which perpetuated India's ancient poverty, as Professor Shenoy and Bauer had warned, for the next half-century. There is a moving and warm tribute here to Shenoy in Bauer's inaugural Shenoy Memorial Lecture.

But Bauer is not merely content with having been vindicated. He has also been interested in explaining the Zeitgeist which produced – and in many cases continues to project – the influential ideas and policies that so totally disregard readily observable reality. It is these reflections, contained in a number of essays in this book, which are likely to resonate with the general reader observing the contemporary world scene.

Bauer's exposure of collective Western guilt, the amputation of the time perspective in our culture and the misuse of language – as noted in a scorching review of Ali Mazrui's Reith Lectures: 'Professor Mazrui's book only confirms that the world language of the late twentieth century is not English: it is Newspeak' – will make all those who wince at the politically correct Blairite project cheer, while his two essays on class and egalitarianism should be compulsory reading for the supporters of Gordon Brown's attack on the 'elitism' of Oxbridge.

My only small quarrel is with Bauer's claim (in the review of Mazrui) that modernisation necessarily implies Westernisation. While this may be true of much of Christian Africa, it is not – as I have recently argued in my *Unintended Consequences* (1998) – of the non-Christian civilisations of Eurasia. As the example of a modernised but non-Westernised Japan shows, it is possible to modernise without adopting the cosmological beliefs of the West. As Bauer himself notes in his essay on Hong Kong, it has modernised spectacularly but, as a colony, eschewed one of the major Western 'habits of the heart' – democracy. The cosmological beliefs underpinning these habits of the heart have been confused in the West, as Bauer rightly notes, because 'of people, clerics included, who have lost their faith. Chesterton predicted long ago that when men cease to believe in a deity, they do not believe in nothing: they then simply believe in anything.' The resulting credulity of the people allows the Western Zeitgeist, castigated so eloquently by Peter Bauer, to develop.

## 8 PETER BAUER'S CONTRIBUTION TO THE DEBATE ON AID TO DEVELOPING COUNTRIES
*Victoria Curzon Price*

Lord Bauer's was a lonely voice when he began studying the economies of former British colonies after World War II, soon to become known as 'development economics'. He favoured markets over government planning, smallholder farming over expensive ventures dreamed up by distant Western experts, individuals over aggregates. He became even lonelier as he began criticising, ever more sharply and with unanswerable logic, what he termed 'the aid industry'. But he lived long enough to see *some* change. The question is: how much?

For instance, if one looks at *Equality, the Third World and Economic Delusion*,[1] published in 1981 and containing what must be one of the severest assessments of 'the aid industry' ever written, one realises that much of what he criticised then is with us still. Hardly anything needs to be changed for readers of a generation later. True, official aid agencies no longer insist on extensive state planning and nowadays extol the virtues of free markets. This is doubtless progress, but the damage is done. As Bauer points out, 'the policies of state-controlled economies in the Third World are not designed to promote development, or to reduce income differences or improve the lot of the poor . . . [but rather] Third World

1    P. T. Bauer, *Equality, the Third World and Economic Delusion*, Weidenfeld and Nicolson, London, 1981.

rulers use economic controls primarily to promote their own political and financial purposes, including the undermining or destroying of opponents and rewarding of supporters' (pp. 105–6). The example of Zimbabwe's current government springs to mind, but there are many others. Why provide official aid to governments that adopt poverty-creating policies? one can hear Lord Bauer asking innocently.

True, most aid recipients no longer actively curtail the inflow and deployment of private foreign capital, but instead seek to promote it. However, after many years of anti-economic policies, bureaucracy and state controls, they often find it difficult to convince foreign investors that they have really changed. After all, the leaders of these countries still use extensive economic controls in order to strengthen and consolidate their grip on their populations, and this will not cease until their system of government itself changes.

True, the World Bank now insists on 'conditionality', unheard of during the cold war. At that time, multilateral aid agencies insisted that no strings should be attached to aid funds since to examine the conduct of recipients would improperly infringe their sovereignty (ibid., p. 95), and even bilateral aid often did nothing to generate any political support for donor governments – raising the question of why they provided the money in the first place. Today, aid and debt relief are often subject to economic and even political conditionality (in terms of supporting the rule of law and human rights, not of politically supporting the donor in the United Nations). But one can imagine Lord Bauer's scepticism. Do we expect aid to dry up if these slippery conditions are not met?

Apart from the three changes noted above, Bauer's analysis of the aid industry of the early post-World War II years needs no modification.

Let us briefly run through some of his main arguments, as convincing today as they ever were.

1. On the burden of indebtedness as a major plank in the advocacy of official aid, and in particular the advocacy of debt cancellation, on the grounds that the burden of debt servicing absorbs a high proportion of export earnings of highly indebted developing countries, Bauer reminds us that the volume of exports depends crucially on the domestic policies of the indebted countries. Difficulties in servicing the debt are clear evidence that capital was either wasted by the recipients or that they refuse to honour their obligations. It therefore follows logically that 'debt cancellation thus favours the incompetent, the improvident and the dishonest' (ibid., p. 96). Furthermore, debt cancellation would not benefit the poorest groups within indebted countries, for these populations are largely outside the exchange economy and have no debts. Those that have debts are the relatively well off, giving rise to the famous Bauerism that aid represents transfers of money from the poor in rich countries to the rich in poor countries.

2. Bauer pours scorn on the notion that material progress in the Third World (or elsewhere for that matter) depends on large investible funds. 'The establishment and improvement of agricultural properties, the building up of small traders' inventories, or the establishment of workshops and small factories requires little finance' (ibid., p. 99). To the aid lobby's argument that developing countries need help because external conditions for development are now so unfavourable (how can they possibly compete with flourishing, dynamic, already entrenched Western firms?), Bauer reminds us that 'economic achievement depends on people's

attributes, attitudes, motivations, mores and political arrangements' (ibid., p. 100) and that, if these conditions for economic development are present, the capital required will either be generated locally or will be willingly lent from abroad. If they are not present, however, aid will be ineffective and wasted.

3. Not only can aid do no good, however. It creates major adverse effects, among which are: the politicisation of life in the Third World (since aid increases the power, resources and patronage of government), the extensive official support of uneconomic activities, large-scale spending on show projects, excessive investment in armies and armaments, the dispossession and persecution of unpopular (but usually economically successful) ethnic minorities and, as a result, the impairment of actual and prospective living standards of ordinary people in poor countries (ibid., p. 105).

4. Bauer returns frequently to the notion that the arguments of the aid industry suggest a barely disguised contempt for Third World countries. The West emerged from poverty by itself, while the Third World cannot do so without massive help ... The poverty of the Third World is the result of Western exploitation, but its chance of a better future depends on Western aid ... To which one might today add: the West has discovered this fantastic complex of institutions called liberal democracy, the rule of law and human rights – the Third World should try them too. But Bauer would probably point out (as he did when discussing the basic requirements for economic achievement) that such attempts to transpose Western institutions 'would require wholesale reform of local beliefs and values, including some of those most deeply felt. Such attempts would involve far-reaching coercion of the supposed

beneficiaries' (ibid., p. 114). Hence Bauer's alarming conclusion that what poses as compassion involves a great deal of condescension, and condescension leads rapidly to coercion (ibid., p. 149).

5. Finally, in this inevitably selective overview of Lord Bauer's thinking on aid, itself only one of his areas of specialisation and research, one should mention his view of the standard argument for aid based on social justice, which may be summarised as follows. If income differences are the result of accident or exploitation, then not only is it *just* that the rich should be taxed to give to the poor, but it is also *costless* (since their wealth is not due to any merit on their part, but theft alone, or mere chance). However, if the economically successful have *created* their wealth, the argument in favour of redistribution fails on grounds of both equity and efficiency. If wealth is created in a positive-sum game, not stolen, income differences are the result of some people being more economically gifted and motivated than others. These are simple human characteristics, among many others, no more in need of being compensated for on grounds of equity than beauty, a good singing voice or sporting ability (should Andre Agassi have his right arm amputated on the grounds of equity?). Furthermore, if taxation reduces motivation, at the margin income redistribution is not costless, because less wealth will be created. This is detrimental to the less economically endowed members of society, since they benefit from their more creative fellows in the form of more choice both in terms of jobs and as consumers.

Although Marxism as a normative, prescriptive policy has failed and indeed is no longer taken seriously by anyone, the positive Marxist assertion that the possession of wealth is the result of exploitation still holds great sway. It is doubtless the most durable of all the fallacies that Lord Bauer spent his long and distinguished career exposing.

## 9  AID, TRADE, DEVELOPMENT: THE BAUER LEGACY
*Razeen Sally*

What makes poor countries 'develop' into rich ones? What keeps them 'underdeveloped'? Does aid work? Is it more important than trade? These questions were the lifelong preoccupation of Peter Bauer. Was he right on development?

For much of the post-war period, development economics had an anti-market, statist bent. The conventional wisdom held that poor countries were beset by huge market failures, particularly a structural gap between investment needs and low rates of domestic saving. Foreign aid was essential to bridge that gap; and it was used to buttress command economy-style planning, state-led industrialisation, nationalisation and protectionism.

There were precious few dissident voices, but among them were Jacob Viner, Gottfried Haberler, Hla Myint and, most prominently, Peter Bauer. In blunt, trenchant language, he rejected socialist planning and recalled the older classical economic virtues of markets and prices as the drivers of economic growth and poverty reduction. Bauer, more than anyone else, must be credited with changing expert thinking on the economics of development – in academia and international organisations, among national donors, and, not least, in developing countries.

Bauer was, above all, a *classical* economist in the tradition of Adam Smith, not a modern, narrowly specialised, technically dazzling neo-classical economist. His basic economic principles are those of *The Wealth of Nations*: government should protect the security of property and persons, but otherwise allow 'natural liberty' – the freedom to produce, exchange and consume according to market prices – free rein. Private enterprise and unimpeded trade, investment and migration in ever-widening markets, not state intervention, are the engines of development.

Moreover, Bauer, like Smith, practised his political economy from the bottom up, closely observing reality at ground level, with a fine sensibility for history, culture and institutions. Not for him the misuse of formal quantitative models in post-war economics, with the concomitant disregard of historical processes and institutional conditions. The young Bauer, it should be recalled, cut his empirical teeth on meticulous pre-independence studies of the rubber industry in Malaya and cocoa production in the Gold Coast (now Ghana). These studies alerted him to the role of small-scale peasant crop-growers and traders, especially how, with the right structures and incentives, they could be entrepreneurial and plan for the long term. His general conclusion was that a combination of light, limited government and the exercise of natural liberty by entrepreneurs big and small, foreign and local, allowed large parts of the developing world to prosper.

To Bauer, trade, not foreign aid, was the handmaiden of development. In the colonial period, particularly through the mediation of the British Empire, extensive and diversified commercial contacts with the West enabled great improvements in the economic well-being of less developed countries – most spectacularly so in the entrepôts of Hong Kong and Singapore. At the other extreme, parts of the world with relatively little contact with the West remained stuck in poverty and misery.

Bauer's classical liberal insights on trade accord with the

recent evidence. Developing countries and now countries in transition with liberal trade policies grow faster and drag more of their people out of poverty than countries which remain protectionist. This is one essential difference between East Asia, eastern Europe and some Latin American countries, on the one hand, and South Asia, the Middle East, the ex-Soviet Union and most of Africa, on the other.

A new World Bank study, for example, concludes that a basket of 24 developing countries, with a total population of three billion, is increasingly integrated into the global economy. These countries have rising absolute and relative shares of manufactures in their total exports; their ratios of trade to national income have doubled since 1980; and the growth of income per head in this group has increased from 1 per cent a year in the 1960s to 5 per cent in the 1990s. The bad news, however, is that about two billion people live in 75 countries with stagnating or declining aggregate growth. This includes virtually all least-developed countries. These happen to be countries that have liberalised less, although they suffer too from other intractable problems, such as poor climate and geography, rampant disease, civil war and chronically corrupt, predatory governments and ruling elites.

Bauer's most controversial writings were on the economics – and politics – of aid. His views can be summed up in this typically blunt sentence: 'government-to-government transfers ... are an excellent method for transferring money from poor people in rich countries to rich people in poor countries'.

Ultimately, aid fails miserably owing to its corrupting psychology and politics. It inculcates the belief that development comes from outside and not through sustained domestic effort. It focuses energies on distributing the spoils of politics rather than on productive wealth creation. It allows venal elites to extract funds through beggary or blackmail – much of it ending up in their pockets or distributed as largesse to political supporters – while perpetuating highly damaging policies at home. Aid thus delays rather than promotes much-needed policy reforms.

Bauer was right: aid has failed. Countries on a drip-feed of aid – for example, sub-Saharan African countries where aid constitutes over 10 per cent of GNP – remain the poorest in the world. Countries with some success in combating poverty, such as India and to a much greater extent China, depend little on aid (less than 1 per cent of GNP in both countries).

Has Bauer won the debate on aid? Not quite. The argument gaining currency today is that more aid is needed and that it does work, provided it goes to countries with a track record of sound market-oriented policies and not to those unable to deliver effective, sustained policy reforms. This is the thrust of the Zedillo Report for the UN, which recommends a doubling of aid to $100 billion annually; of the recent UN Monterrey Declaration; of the Melzer Commission Report for the US Congress, which recommends that aid (in the form of grants) should be diverted from middle-income to low-income countries; of President Mbeki's new initiative on aid and development for Africa; and of President Bush's recent decision to increase US aid by $5 billion over three years.

In economic terms, there is perhaps a case for increased aid in support of market-promoting reforms, to part-finance infrastructure (for instance, basic education, primary health care and rural roads), and to combat endemic tropical diseases (such as malaria and HIV/Aids) in the world's poorest countries. This, though, is not nearly as important as trade liberalisation in developing countries and in highly protected Western markets for agriculture and textiles.

However, Bauer's siren voice on the inherent politics and psychology of aid should make one exceedingly sceptical of grand aid-expanding initiatives, even though they enjoy the imprimatur of prominent economic liberals such as ex-President Zedillo of Mexico. Most aid still goes to corrupt, criminal governments. National and international aid bureaucracies, in alliance with assorted consultants, academics and NGOs, have a vested interest in the aid business, mostly with little regard to policy results. Rather than showering more manna on the aid circus, wouldn't it be better to restructure the existing $50 billion of annual aid so that it goes to deserving countries with improving policies?

Lord Bauer wanted to be remembered not so much for original theories and insights but for clarity of thought and moral courage. Swimming vigorously against the intellectual tides of his time, he repeated the enduring verities of Adam Smith and applied them to the post-war developing world. 'Let us be free from cant' was his motto; and he was fond of this quote from Pascal: 'Let us labour at thinking clearly. Herein lies the source of moral conduct.' This is indeed how Lord Bauer, a true child of the Scottish Enlightenment, should be remembered.

## 10 PETER BAUER AND INDIA
*Parth J. Shah*


I first spoke to Lord Bauer in June 1997 about my plans to start a free-market think tank in India. I was teaching economics at the time in the US, and Alex Chafuen (Atlas Foundation) and John Blundell (IEA) had both suggested that I should contact him given his long-standing interest in India. Despite his ill health, he sounded happy and excited by the prospects, reminisced about his visits to India, and readily agreed to join the Board of Scholars of the Centre for Civil Society. He was the first member of the board, even before the Centre was officially registered in New Delhi. He was a steadfast supporter thereafter.

Lord Bauer wrote two books specifically on India: *United States Aid and Indian Economic Development*, 1959, and *Indian Economic Policy and Development*, 1965 (first published in London in 1961). The books dealt head-on with the views of the Indian intelligentsia and the numerous international advisers who saw India as a laboratory for combining economic central planning with a democratic polity. Harold Laski, Nicholas Kaldor, Joan Robinson, John Strachey, Oskar Lange, Michael Kalecki and Gunnar Myrdal all participated in the Indian experiment – the experiment for which the poor paid the most. By challenging their views on industrialisation through large-scale manufacturing and the neglect of trade and agriculture, forced saving, foreign aid, failures of the market, the miracle of planning, and population as the problem,

Lord Bauer became the true friend of the poor of India, and of the world.

The popular theory of the 'vicious circle of poverty' held that low incomes did not leave much for saving, leading to lack of investment and growth. Without the aid to break the vicious circle, the theory maintained, no development was possible. Bauer demolished the theory with the simple observation that, if it were true, humankind would still be living in caves! Not only was the theory justifying aid false, but the practical effects were also unfavourable. Aid (he called it government-to-government transfers) strengthened the state over the private sector by giving it more resources, allowed it to build prestige monuments which were copies of the grand projects in the West (he called this the international demonstration effect), and supported dirigiste policies to no end. The history of Western aid has proved him absolutely right.

Bauer's second book on India contains a large number of real-life observations that substantiate the Hayekian thesis on the role of dispersed and inarticulate knowledge and the rationale for 'Why the Worst Get on Top' during politicisation of the economy. His accounts there foreshadow the development of formal theories on rent-seeking and public choice. His explanation for widespread beggary in India is truly perceptive: 'Hinduism and Islam, the two principal religions [of India], encourage begging, since they enjoin their followers to support beggars.' Beggars in India, Bauer observed, are not a sign of national poverty, but of religious ethos. People maim themselves in order to earn as beggars, though more often they are disfigured by the mafia that controls prime begging sites in the cities. Beggary is an industry in India!

Government-directed development was the only option, it was argued, because India lacked resources, capital, and management and entrepreneurial skills necessary for large factories and infrastructure projects. Bauer aptly retorted: central planning does not augment resources but only creates and concentrates power. The capital gets diverted from the private to the public sector; no new capital is created just by using planning as opposed to the price system. He documented that, given the state of India's development at the time, small capital investments in agriculture would be more effective than large investments in massive factories and dams. By improving the productivity of the marginal farmer, the resultant development would also be more equitable.

If the people lacked the requisite management and entrepreneurial skills, how would the staff of government agencies possess them? Was the Indian government going to be run by officials from other countries or planets? Besides, at the time of independence, India was a major importer not of textiles but of textile machinery. It had private steel mills, an airline, and even electricity generators.

Unfortunately for India, Bauer's proofs and pleadings fell on dogmatic ears. He first visited India in 1958, in the immediate aftermath of the Second Five Year Plan that was to establish a 'socialist pattern of society' through state control of the 'commanding heights of the economy'. The Forum of Free Enterprise, the first free-market think tank started by A. D. Shroff in 1956 in Bombay, hosted his two public lectures on 'Economic Progress of Under-Developed Countries' on 8 and 9 September. The Forum published those lectures under the title *Some Economic Aspects and Problems of Under-Developed Countries* later that year. Bauer came to India several times between 1958 and 1982. Each time, the Forum, later under the leadership of M. R. Pai, provided him a public platform and published his talks: *Reflections on Foreign Aid*, *Central Planning and Economic Development*, *The Market in the Dock*, *The Concept of Economic Equality*, to list a few. Lord Bauer's last trip to India was in March 1993 to deliver the B. R. Shenoy Memorial Lecture at Ahmedabad, Gujarat.

Bauer first learned about Professor Shenoy through the documents of the Second Five Year Plan, as an author of the one-man Note of Dissent to the Plan. He probably would not otherwise have met him, since official circles had declared Shenoy a 'madman'. He was completely ignored in the corridors of power, and was 'untouchable'. They developed a friendship and became comrades in arms to fight against the prevailing orthodoxy. Shenoy and Bauer were joined by Milton Friedman – the group of three, as Deepak Lal points out, who tried their best to persuade India to turn its back on the permit-quota raj.

Milton Friedman first came to India in the autumn of 1955 as an adviser to the Ministry of Finance, recommended by the Eisenhower administration. He wrote a long memorandum which the government never published, critiquing the Draft Second Five Year Plan. He continued his battle during the 1963 visit by writing in newspapers and magazines and by talking with the Forum audience. (The memorandum and an unpublished 1963 paper are in *Friedman on India*, Centre for Civil Society, 2000.)

Most of Bauer's ideas are now part of the common wisdom, though his message regarding the 'unholy grail of economic equality' is still not fully understood, in India and elsewhere. Bauer's work ingeniously combines economics with history, anthropology and sociology, all of these buttressed by his keen sense of observation. Development economics is now moving along these multidisciplinary lines, which Bauer trod long ago. But his powers of observation would be impossible to match.

The place that Bauer last visited in India to deliver the B. R. Shenoy Memorial Lecture, Ahmedabad, has a Harold Laski Institute. It would be most fitting if it were to be converted to the Peter Bauer Institute. Bauer understood India far better and suggested the right path for progress.

## 11 PETER BAUER:
## SOME RECOLLECTIONS
*Alan Walters*

Together with Sally, he came to our house for lunch on 24 March 2002. He remarked that at 86 he was near blind, somewhat deaf, unable to walk more than a tentative step or two and practically wheelchair-bound. Yet Paddie and I were both convinced that, in spite of the difficulties of communication, he displayed still that constantly enquiring mind always associated with Peter. In fact both of us agreed that it seemed as though his health had improved over the last month or so. And he had interesting views on the current Middle East conflict.

Now that he has gone, we can reflect on Peter's gifts. By any measure they were awesome. Who can say which are his most important contributions to scholarship? Who can adequately assess his fundamental challenge to the prevailing orthodoxy? None of us, I fear. We are too near.

Yet we can recall the man and his works, however inadequate the *raccontatore*. I had the privilege of collaborating, as very much a junior partner, in three (or four, depending on the count!) articles broadly on the state of economics. The theme was that economics was making great progress with ever more sophisticated theory and techniques. One area of economics after another had been taken over through the use of mathematics and the non-mathematical reader was exiled from discussion.

Peter memorably described the situation as rather like the

middle years of the Roman empire. The legions of Rome were still conquering the barbarians and expanding and defending the empire. But at the centre, in Rome, the institutions were decaying and the fundamental principles of civilised conduct were being increasingly flouted.

Just so, the most distinguished economists, by neglecting the elementary principles of economics as developed in the laws of demand and supply, made the most elementary errors in analysis and policies. Of course, Peter had many examples of such neglect in the field of development economics. However, the most surprising example was the so-called 'dollar shortage' of the 1940s and early 1950s. The cream of the economics profession announced that there would always be a dollar shortage because of the permanent excess demand for the exports of the United States. Changes in monetary and fiscal policy were completely ignored (except notably by Friedman and Haberler).

I fondly recall what a pleasure it was to co-author articles with Peter, who was almost pedantic in his need to be precise in his use of language. (His critics have largely retired perhaps none the wiser but a little better informed.) All the texts of our articles were subject to the most rigorous analysis to see whether they would stand a robustness test; not a sloppy word or sentence would escape his perusal.

But writing with Peter was a social occasion – usually lunch or dinner in Montague Square accompanied our efforts. Alas, during the later years we could not fully reconstruct the pleasures of the past. We had all got older. Now all we have is our memories.

## 12 COLLABORATING WITH PETER BAUER
*Basil Yamey*

Peter Bauer's work on British West Africa was conducted under the auspices of the Colonial Economic Research Committee (of which Arnold Plant was a leading member) and financed with a grant from the Colonial Office. He was engaged to investigate the structure of West African trade, and especially of monopolistic tendencies. Peter's work began in 1949; and his book *West African Trade* was published five years later. It is a large book of more than 400 pages. It is now recognised as a classic. By 1951/2 Peter had collected a mass of material: reports, books, statistical tabulations, pieces of paper with his handwritten notes, typed outlines and numerous thin exercise books in which he scribbled thoughts and ideas. What was worse from the narrow point of view of organisation was that, in addition, Peter's mind was full of information he had gathered but not written down, as well as yet more ideas and plans. I doubt whether he missed anything of significance for his investigation on his visits to West Africa. Throughout his working life he had the remarkable ability to see the significance of what superficially may have seemed rather trivial. West African examples include traders reselling imported scent sometimes by the drop, and the practice known as gold-coasting (an African trader buying goods from a wholesaler on long credit, and reselling them almost immediately for cash at lower prices).

Peter felt that he could not on his own turn all this into a well-ordered and effective book. Ronald Coase suggested to him that I might be willing to help. Peter and I had been colleagues at the LSE in 1948. By 1951 I had read his papers on the British agricultural marketing boards and also his book on the rubber-growing industry and its regulation. I was interested and impressed by these careful and well-argued studies. We met and Peter gave me some idea of what he had in mind. It sounded fascinating. I was, I recall, especially interested in his thoughts on the role of traders – large wholesalers as well as petty sedentary and itinerant traders. My father and several of his contemporaries had begun their working lives as small-scale traders in South Africa, and I was aware of their contributions, small individually, to the improvement of the lot of farmers and others in the rural areas.

So we started. We worked at my house in Hampstead Garden Suburb, mostly over weekends, when Peter would stay overnight. No time was 'wasted', but we remained closeted in the study, refreshed by cups of coffee bought in by the au pair, who was in awe of the distinguished-looking visitor concentrating his attention on papers or on arguing with me. My wife Helen insisted, though, that we went with her for a longish walk on the Heath before Sunday lunch.

After I had worked my way into the material, we had planning sessions – though I am sure we avoided that word. We called it drawing up the order of battle for the book as a whole and for each chapter. Like good or bad generals, we frequently revised the orders of battle, even during the galley-proof stage. Then the drafting started, with me doing the writing – a necessary division of labour in the light of Peter's hieroglyphic writing. Each paragraph was drafted and frequently revised; and this was at a time before the word-processor. (Fortunately, the highly efficient Mrs Margaret

97

Jones lived near by, and provided successive typecripts.) We argued; we criticised each other's suggestions and ideas; and neither of us would approve a paragraph until completely satisfied with the analysis and presentation. I believe we did achieve a fairly satisfactory simple joint style and a reasonable clarity of exposition. The latter achievement was the more difficult in that together we did our best to forestall possible counter-arguments; and this invariably reduced the pace and disturbed the smoothness of the exposition. One thing I am sure we did largely accomplish: that is, we ruthlessly pruned the final version of any words and phrases that one or other of us was inclined to use excessively. While working on the book, we also wrote some articles which were based in large measure on material being included in the book. These were published as jointly authored articles in academic journals.

We enjoyed working together. It was fun as well as hard work and long hours. More important, we each realised that the resolution of our friendly disagreements on questions of analysis and interpretation helped to refine and improve our ideas and our understanding of the issues we were dealing with. It also, of course, increased our academic 'productivity', certainly in quantity, and I hope in quality.

So when Milton Friedman and C. W. Guillebaud, as joint editors, invited us to write a book in the Cambridge Economic Handbooks series on the economics of underdeveloped countries, we agreed to do so, though we did have serious misgivings. It was a difficult slog, and far less rewarding, in non-pecuniary terms, than the work on the West Africa book. Nevertheless, we finished the manuscript more or less on schedule; and the book, reprinted several times and translated into about half a dozen languages, was mildly rewarding in pecuniary terms.

We continued to work together on various articles and collections of articles until the late 1980s. Peter was always eager to return to a subject, such as foreign aid or population, whenever he had new ideas or had thought of better ways of presenting his ideas. But eventually, after several unsuccessful promptings by me, he told me he had finally decided to stop writing for publication, whether by himself or jointly with me. I expressed my disbelief. He had made similar declarations before. This time, though, he was serious. He showed me a solemn and binding written undertaking, on House of Lords paper, to the effect that he would not write another article. (He signed it, and attached a mock seal. There was only one lapse – a minor one, made for a highly persuasive reason.)

On several occasions Peter thanked me publicly for the help I had given him in the course of our collaboration. I am pleased to say, here, that his friendship and our collaboration meant much to me.

# ABOUT THE IEA

The Institute is a research and educational charity (No. CC 235 351), limited by guarantee. Its mission is to improve understanding of the fundamental institutions of a free society with particular reference to the role of markets in solving economic and social problems.

The IEA achieves its mission by:

- a high-quality publishing programme
- conferences, seminars, lectures and other events
- outreach to school and college students
- brokering media introductions and appearances

The IEA, which was established in 1955 by the late Sir Antony Fisher, is an educational charity, not a political organisation. It is independent of any political party or group and does not carry on activities intended to affect support for any political party or candidate in any election or referendum, or at any other time. It is financed by sales of publications, conference fees and voluntary donations.

In addition to its main series of publications the IEA also publishes a quarterly journal, *Economic Affairs*, and has two specialist programmes – Environment and Technology, and Education.

The IEA is aided in its work by a distinguished international Academic Advisory Council and an eminent panel of Honorary Fellows. Together with other academics, they review prospective IEA publications, their comments being passed on anonymously to authors. All IEA papers are therefore subject to the same rigorous independent refereeing process as used by leading academic journals.

IEA publications enjoy widespread classroom use and course adoptions in schools and universities. They are also sold throughout the world and often translated/reprinted.

Since 1974 the IEA has helped to create a world-wide network of 100 similar institutions in over 70 countries. They are all independent but share the IEA's mission.

Views expressed in the IEA's publications are those of the authors, not those of the Institute (which has no corporate view), its Managing Trustees, Academic Advisory Council members or senior staff.

Members of the Institute's Academic Advisory Council, Honorary Fellows, Trustees and Staff are listed on the following page.

The Institute gratefully acknowledges financial support for its publications programme and other work from a generous benefaction by the late Alec and Beryl Warren.

Other papers recently published by the IEA include:

## WHO, What and Why?

*Transnational Government, Legitimacy and the World Health Organization*
Roger Scruton
Occasional Paper 113; ISBN 0 255 36487 3
£8.00

## The World Turned Rightside Up

*A New Trading Agenda for the Age of Globalisation*
John C. Hulsman
Occasional Paper 114; ISBN 0 255 36495 4
£8.00

## The Representation of Business in English Literature

Introduced and edited by Arthur Pollard
Readings 53; ISBN 0 255 36491 1
£12.00

## Anti-Liberalism 2000

*The Rise of New Millennium Collectivism*
David Henderson
Occasional Paper 115; ISBN 0 255 36497 0
£7.50

## The Changing Fortunes of Economic Liberalism

*Yesterday, Today and Tomorrow*
David Henderson
Occasional Paper 105 (new edition); ISBN 0 255 36520 9
£12.50

## The Global Education Industry

*Lessons from Private Education in Developing Countries*
James Tooley
Hobart Paper 141 (new edition); ISBN 0 255 36503 9
£12.50

## Saving Our Streams

*The Role of the Anglers' Conservation Association in*
*Protecting English and Welsh Rivers*
Roger Bate
Research Monograph 53; ISBN 0 255 36494 6
£10.00

## Better Off Out?

*The Benefits or Costs of EU Membership*
Brian Hindley & Martin Howe
Occasional Paper 99 (new edition); ISBN 0 255 36502 0
£10.00

## Buckingham at 25

*Freeing the Universities from State Control*
Edited by James Tooley
Readings 55; ISBN 0 255 36512 8
£15.00


## Lectures on Regulatory and Competition Policy

Irwin M. Stelzer
Occasional Paper 120; ISBN 0 255 36511 X
£12.50


## Misguided Virtue

*False Notions of Corporate Social Responsibility*
David Henderson
Hobart Paper 142; ISBN 0 255 36510 1
£12.50


## HIV and Aids in Schools

*The Political Economy of Pressure Groups and Miseducation*
Barrie Craven, Pauline Dixon, Gordon Stewart & James Tooley
Occasional Paper 121; ISBN 0 255 36522 5
£10.00

## The Road to Serfdom

*The* Reader's Digest *condensed version*
Friedrich A. Hayek
Occasional Paper 122; ISBN 0 255 36530 6
£7.50


## Bastiat's *The Law*

Introduction by Norman Barry
Occasional Paper 123; ISBN 0 255 36509 8
£7.50


## A Globalist Manifesto for Public Policy

Charles Calomiris
Occasional Paper 124; ISBN 0 255 36525 X
£7.50


## Euthanasia for Death Duties

*Putting Inheritance Tax Out of Its Misery*
Barry Bracewell-Milnes
Research Monograph 54; ISBN 0 255 36513 6
£10.00

## Liberating the Land

*The Case for Private Land-use Planning*
Mark Pennington
Hobart Paper 143; ISBN 0 255 36508 x
£10.00


## IEA Yearbook of Government Performance 2002/ 2003

Edited by Peter Warburton
Yearbook 1; ISBN 0 255 36532 2
£15.00


## Britain's Relative Economic Performance, 1870– 1999

Nicholas Crafts
Research Monograph 55; ISBN 0 255 36524 1
£10.00


## Should We Have Faith in Central Banks?

Otmar Issing
Occasional Paper 125; ISBN 0 255 36528 4
£7.50

## The Dilemma of Democracy

Arthur Seldon

Hobart Paper 136 (reissue); ISBN 0 255 36536 5

£10.00

## Capital Controls: a 'Cure' Worse Than the Problem?

Forrest Capie

Research Monograph 56; ISBN 0 255 36506 3

£10.00

## The Poverty of 'Development Economics'

Deepak Lal

Hobart Paper 144 (reissue); ISBN 0 255 36519 5

£15.00

## Should Britain Join the Euro?

*The Chancellor's Five Tests Examined*

Patrick Minford

Occasional Paper 126; ISBN 0 255 36527 6

£7.50

## Post-Communist Transition: Some Lessons

Leszek Balcerowicz

Occasional Paper 127; ISBN 0 255 36533 0

£7.50

To order copies of currently available IEA papers, or to enquire about availability, please write (no postage required from within the UK) to:

Lavis Marketing
IEA orders
FREEPOST LON21280
Oxford OX3 7BR

Or contact Lavis Marketing on:
Tel: 01865 767575
Fax: 01865 750079
Email: orders@lavismarketing.co.uk

The IEA also offers a subscription service to its publications. For a single annual payment, currently £40.00 in the UK, you will receive every title the IEA publishes across the course of a year, invitations to events, and discounts on our extensive back catalogue. For more information, please contact:

Subscriptions
The Institute of Economic Affairs
2 Lord North Street
London SW1P 3LB

Tel: 020 7799 8900
Fax: 020 7799 2137
Website: www.iea.org.uk